BASIC BIBLE
DOCTRINES

OF THE
CHRISTIAN FAITH

WHAT IS HELL?

Edward D. Andrews

i

WHAT IS HELL?

Basic Bible Doctrines of the Christian Faith

Edward D. Andrews

Christian Publishing House
Professional Christian Publishing of the Good News

support@christianpublishers.org

Write support@christianpublishers.org

ISBN-13: **978-0692610176**

ISBN-10: **0692610170**

Christian Publishing House

Cambridge, Ohio

WHAT IS HELL? Basic Bible Doctrines of the Christian Faith

Bible Translations Referred to in This Book

Unless otherwise indicated, Scripture quotations are from the *English Standard Version of the Holy Scriptures*, 2001 (*ESV*). Abbreviations used to designate other translations of the Bible are provided below:

ASV -- American Standard Version (1901) Public Domain

AMP -- Amplified Bible (1987) The Lockman Foundation

AT -- The Bible--An American Translation (1935), J. M. Powis Smith and Edgar J. Goodspeed.

CEV -- Contemporary English Version (1995) American Bible Society

DARBY -- Darby Translation (1890) Public Domain

GNT -- Good News Translation (1966, 1971, 1976, 1992) American Bible Society

HCSB -- Holman Christian Standard Bible (2003) Holman Bible Publishers.

JB -- The Jerusalem Bible (1966), Alexander Jones, general editor.

JP -- The Holy Scriptures According to the Masoretic Text (1917), Jewish Publication Society of America.

KJV -- King James Version (1611, 1942). Public Domain

LEB -- Lexham English Bible (LEB) Logos Bible Software

LXX -- Greek Septuagint Version of Hebrew Old Testament (280-150 B.C.E.).

NTB -- A New Translation of the Bible (1934), James Moffatt.

NASB -- New American Standard Bible (1960, 1962, 1963, 1968, 1971, 1972, 1973, 1975, 1977, 1995) The Lockman Foundation[1]

NET -- New English Translation (2006) Biblical Studies Press

NIV -- New International Version (2011) Biblica, Inc.

NLT -- New Living Translation (2007) Tyndale House Foundation

TEB -- The Emphasised Bible (1897), Joseph B. Rotherham.

RSV -- Revised Standard Version, Second Edition (1971). Division of Christian Education of the National Council of the Churches

UASV – Updated American Standard Version (Expected release 2018) Christian Publishing House

---

[1] http://www.lockman.org

WHNU -- Westcott-Hort Greek New Testament / Nestle-Aland Creek New Testament, United Bible Society Greek New Testament (1881, 2012, and 1993)

YLT -- Young's Literal Translation (1887) Public Domain

INTRODUCTION What Really Is Hell?

When the word "hell" is mentioned, many people have different images that come to mind. However, for most Christians the general consensus is the same. For them, "hell" is a place of eternal torment, i.e., a place of punishment for sinners. These have heard this their entire lives, so anyone that would say otherwise is dismissed as a heretic worse case scenario or not a true conservative Christian best case scenario. Let us offer a few biblical reasons within this short introduction chapter as to why the reader should consider the other side of the story, i.e., eternal destruction as opposed to eternal torment. Later chapters will dig deeper, making the case for eternal destruction. Thus, this introduction should, at least, offer the motivation for reading the rest of the book.

FIRST, let us start with Paul, who as we know was known as Saul before becoming the apostle Paul. Nevertheless, the objective way of believing certain Bible doctrines as being the truth is as follows. The biblical view of the doctrine _____ is _____, and it is the truth, unless, enough evidence comes along to say otherwise. If we grow in knowledge and understanding, our conclusions based on previous knowledge may need to be revised. For increased knowledge can require adjustments in one's thinking. We must remember the Apostle Paul studied under the renowned Pharisee Gamaliel, who was the grandson of Hillel, the Elder (110 B.C.E.[2] – 10 C.E.), the founder of one of the two schools within Judaism. Paul describes himself as "circumcised on the eighth day, of the people of Israel, of the tribe of Benjamin, a Hebrew of Hebrews; as to the law, a Pharisee; as to zeal, a persecutor of the church; as to righteousness under the law, blameless." (Phil 3:5-6) He also states, "But whatever gain I had, I counted as loss for the sake of Christ. Indeed, I count everything as loss because of the surpassing worth of knowing Christ Jesus my Lord. For his sake I have suffered the loss of all things and count them as rubbish, in order that I may gain Christ" (Phil. 3:7-8) Thus, we know that the Israelites were God's chosen people and the only way to God for some 1,500 years. However, Jesus brought a new way, Christianity. Saul/Paul was slow to accept this because he could not see Jesus Christ as the long-awaited Messiah. Nevertheless, after Jesus visited Paul on the road to Damascus and Ananias, a Christian disciple of Damascus, visited Paul, he saw the Old Testament Scriptures pointing to the Messiah accurately, he was able to humble himself and accept a different belief, i.e., Christianity was the truth and the way.

To believe without enough support, to believe in the face of contrary evidence is irrational.

---

[2] B.C.E. years ran down toward zero, although the Romans had no zero, and C.E. years ran up from zero. (100, 10, 3, 2, 1 ◀B.C.E. | C.E.▶ 1, 2, 3, 10, and 100)

Therefore, we must humbly examine the facts behind what we believe, to establish the truth continually. Just as the apostle Paul exhorted the Christians at Corinth to "examine yourselves, to see whether you are in the faith. Test yourselves" (2 Cor. 13:5), we could say the very same thing about our beliefs. We could say, 'examine our beliefs, to see whether they are the truth, test our beliefs.' Now, this is not to suggest that our beliefs are to be ever changing, but that they should be able to stand up to scrutiny when they are challenged by something we have heard or read. However, this refinement of our beliefs should not be confused with allowing unfounded, damaging doubts to grow in our hearts and minds, doubts that can destroy our confidently established beliefs and our relationship with our heavenly Father. **Unfounded doubt** is defined as something that is not supported by any evidence or a minuscule amount of evidence, to cause uncertainty of belief or opinion that often interferes with our decision-making skills.

SECOND, we need to dig deeper into biblical truths, not as a sign of unfounded doubt but to make sure what we believe is so. If we believe that we can survive off the basic Bible knowledge that we acquired in the beginning and the simple snacks we receive at each Christian meeting, we are sadly mistaken because our spiritual health will deteriorate. It would be similar to our believing that we could maintain our physical health by simply eating here and there.

Acts 17:10-11 Updated American Standard Version (UASV)

Paul and Silas in Berea

10 The brothers immediately sent Paul and Silas away by night to Berea, and when they arrived, they went into the synagogue of the Jews. 11 Now these were more noble-minded than those in Thessalonica, for they received the word with great eagerness, examining the Scriptures daily to see whether these things were so.

Note that they **(1)** "received the word with all eagerness," and then went about **(2)** "examining the Scriptures daily to see if these things were so." If the apostle Paul was to be examined to see if what he said was so, surely uninspired commentators must be examined as well.

1 Timothy 1:13 Updated American Standard Version (UASV)

13 although formerly I [Saul/Paul] was a blasphemer, and a persecutor, and a violent man. But I was shown mercy because I had acted unknowingly with a lack of trust,

Romans 10:2-3 Updated American Standard Version (UASV)

2 For I [Saul/Paul] bear them witness that they [the Jews] have a zeal for God, but not according to

accurate knowledge.[3] **3** For, being ignorant of the righteousness of God, and seeking to establish their own, they did not submit to God's righteousness.

What has been demonstrated here thus far? Just because one is very active in their Christian denomination or church, this activity does not guarantee that they are receiving God's approval or that they are doctrinally correct. See Jesus words below for those who believed that they were in an approved relationship. It takes real heart and character to accept that one may be on the wrong path when it comes to long held biblical beliefs. It takes an act of humility to accept that we may need to make an adjustment in our view of a certain doctrine.

Matthew 7:21-23 Updated American Standard Version (UASV)

21 "Not everyone who says to me, 'Lord, Lord,' will enter the kingdom of heaven, but the one who does the will of my Father who is in heaven. **22** On that day many will say to me, 'Lord, Lord, did we not prophesy in your name, and cast out demons in your name, and do many mighty works in your name?' **23** And then I will declare to them, 'I never knew you; depart from me, you who practice lawlessness.'

---

[3] *Epignosis* is a strengthened or intensified form of *gnosis* (*epi*, meaning "additional"), meaning, "true," "real," "full," "complete" or "accurate," depending upon the context. Paul and Peter alone use *epignosis*.

It was Saul/Paul's zeal and his conscience that was pricked to defend what he thought was the truth, and yet he clearly admitted that his was over-zealous, that his zeal was misdirected, because of ignorance. This should cause us to pause and reflect. The presence of false teachers in the Christian congregation from the first century onward means that one cannot just accept naively that they are getting the truth. It would be foolish to assume such.

1 Thessalonians 5:21 Updated American Standard Version (UASV)

²¹ But examine everything carefully; hold fast to that which is good;

The Greek word *dokimazete* rendered simply as "test" in the English Standard Version or the Holman Christian Standard Bible denotes a careful examination of "everything." If one is to make a careful examination of everything, it will require that they are not just passively going along, but rather, one should be buying out the time, to have an accurate understanding of God's Word, by doing an in-depth study of what they believe to be true.

Certainly, if what Paul had to say about the Scriptures was under examination, no one else is above having their beliefs examined. The Jews of Berea did not just accept what Paul was saying about the death and resurrection of Jesus, as being so. Moreover, Paul commended them for their due diligence. (See 17:3) This was no brief or superficial examination of the Scriptures either; they met daily to examine the Scriptures. For the above reasons, it is only through living by faith and accurate knowledge that we can receive God's favor.

Examine Everything Carefully

When we are considering what the punishment is for sin, Scripture is the final authority. However, we do not want to delve off into inappropriate proof-texting, which is the practice of using isolated Scripture quotations, out of context, from the Bible to establish a particular doctrinal position. Note that proof texting in and of itself is not wrong. It is only wrong if we do it out of context, which causes us to end up with what we believe the text is saying rather than what the authors meant by their own words.

Romans 5:12 Updated American Standard Version (UASV)

[12] Therefore, just as through one man sin entered into the world, and death through sin, and so death spread to all men, because all sinned,

In the above text, Paul addresses sin and its effect. In the same book, he goes on to write, "For the wages of sin is death, but the free gift[4] of God is eternal life in Christ Jesus our Lord." (Rom. 6:23, UASV) Paul under inspiration tells us that the punishment for sin is death, which leads to the

---

[4] Lit *gracious gift*; Gr *kharisma*

questions, how are we to understand the word "hell" in the face of this revelation? What is hell? What do the Hebrew and Greek words behind the English rendering "hell" (Sheol, Hades, Gehenna, and Tartarus) really mean? After the death of a person, does life of some kind, in some form continue? After determining what hell is, we must then decide who goes there. Moreover, does the Bible offer any hope for those in hell? All of this and far more will be addressed throughout this publication.

CHAPTER 1 Hellfire - Eternal Torment?

Hundreds of millions of both Catholic and Protest Christians have long held that hell is a place of eternal torment for the damned. According to the Encarta Encyclopedia, "Hell, in theology, any place or state of punishment and privation for human souls after death. More strictly, the term is applied to the place or state of eternal punishment of the damned, whether angels or human beings. The doctrine of the existence of hell is derived from the principle of the necessity for the vindication of divine justice, combined with the human experience that evildoers do not always appear to be punished adequately in their lifetime. Belief in a hell was widespread in antiquity and is found in most religions of the world today."

However, it would seem that hellfire and brimstone have lost their spark. The same encyclopedia goes on to say, "In modern times the belief in physical punishment after death and the endless duration of this punishment has been rejected by many. The question about the nature of the punishment of hell is equally controversial. Opinions range from holding the pains of hell to be no more than the remorse of conscience to the traditional belief that the "pain of loss" (the consciousness of having forfeited the vision of God and the happiness of heaven) is combined with the "pain of sense" (actual physical torment).[5]

Probably the most famous hellfire and brimstone preacher was Jonathan Edwards (1703-1758), used to put the fear of God into the hearts and minds of the 18th-century Colonial Americans with detail, explicit, lifelike, word pictures of hell

"Sinners in the Hands of an Angry God" Known for his fiery sermons, clergyman Jonathan Edwards helped start the Great Awakening, an American religious revival of the 1740s.

> The God that holds you over the pit of hell, much as one holds a spider, or some loathsome insect over the fire, abhors you, and is dreadfully provoked: his wrath towards you burns like fire; he looks upon you as worthy of nothing else, but to be cast into the fire; he is of purer eyes than to bear to have you in his sight; you are ten thousand times more abominable in his eyes, than the most hateful venomous serpent is in ours. You have offended him infinitely more than ever a stubborn rebel did his prince; and yet it is nothing but his hand that holds you from falling into the fire every moment.

---

[5] Microsoft ® Encarta ® 2006. © 1993-2005 Microsoft Corporation. All rights reserved.

O sinner! Consider the fearful danger you are in: it is a great furnace of wrath, a wide and bottomless pit, full of the fire of wrath, that you are held over in the hand of that God, whose wrath is provoked and incensed as much against you, as against many of the damned in hell. You hang by a slender thread, with the flames of divine wrath flashing about it, and ready every moment to singe it, and burn it asunder;[6]

Like Edwards, many other Catholic and Protestant preachers, say that God has this eternal place in the offing for the wicked. However, what does the Bible really teach?

Hell

Without being bogged down in doctrinal issues, let us just deal with the facts. "Hell" is the English translation for the Hebrew word Sheol and the Greek word Hades. Therefore, we need not ask, what Hell is. However, what did the word mean when it was first placed in English translations? Webster's Eleventh New International Dictionary, under "Hell" says: [Middle English, from Old English; akin to Old English helan to conceal, Old High German helan, Latin celare, Greek kalyptein]

---

[6] Edwards, Jonathan (2010-05-20). Sinners In The Hands Of An Angry God (Kindle Locations 151-152). Old Land Mark Publishing. Kindle Edition.

before 12th century"[7] The word "hell" meant to 'cover' over or 'conceal,' so it would have meant a place 'covered' or 'concealed,' such as a grave.

Sheol

Webster's Dictionary, "[Hebrew Shĕ'ōl] 1597: the abode of the dead in early Hebrew thought"[8] Collier's Encyclopedia (1986, Vol. 12, p. 28) says: "Since Sheol in Old Testament times referred simply to the abode of the dead and suggested no moral distinctions, the word 'hell,' as understood today, is not a happy translation." Some translations choose to use a transliteration, Sheol, as opposed to the English hell, AT, RSV, ESV, LEB, HCSB, and NASB.

Hades

Everyone knows that Hades was "the underground abode of the dead in Greek mythology."[9] However, as far as early Christianity,

---

[7] Frederick C. Mish, "Preface," *Merriam-Webster's Collegiate Dictionary.* (Springfield, MA: Merriam-Webster, Inc., 2003). hell

[8] Frederick C. Mish, "Preface," *Merriam-Webster's Collegiate Dictionary.* (Springfield, MA: Merriam-Webster, Inc., 2003). sheol

[9] Frederick C. Mish, "Preface," *Merriam-Webster's Collegiate Dictionary.* (Springfield, MA: Merriam-Webster, Inc., 2003). hades

the Greek translation of the Old Testament, the Septuagint, uses the word Hades 73 times, employing it 60 times to translate the Hebrew word Sheol. Luke at Acts 2:27 write, "For you will not abandon my soul to Hades, or let your Holy One see corruption." Luke was quoting Psalm 16:10, which reads, "For you will not abandon my soul to Sheol, or let your holy one see corruption." Notice that Luke used Hades in place of Sheol. Therefore, Hades is the Greek equivalent of Sheol, as far as Christians and the Greek New Testament is concerned. In other words, Hades is also the abode of the dead in early Christian thought. Some translations choose to use a transliteration, Hades, as opposed to the English hell, ASV, AT, RSV, ESV, LEB, HCSB, and NASB.

Gehenna

Gehenna Hebrew Ge' Hinnom, literally, valley of Hinnom appears 12 times in the Greek New Testament books, and many translators render it by the word "hell." Most translations have chosen poorly not to use a transliteration, Gehenna or Geenna, as opposed to the English hell, ASV, AT, RSV, ESV, LEB, HCSB, and NASB. There is little doubt that the New Testament writers and Jesus used "Gehenna" to speak of the place of final punishment. What was Gehenna?

According to the Holman Illustrated Bible Dictionary (p. 632), Gehenna or the Valley of Hinnom was "the valley south of Jerusalem now called the Wadi er-Rababi (Josh. 15:8; 18:16; 2 Chron. 33:6; Jer. 32:35) became the place of child sacrifice to foreign gods. The Jews later used the valley for the dumping of refuse, the dead bodies of animals, and executed criminals."[10] We would disagree with the other comments by the Holman Illustrated Dictionary, "The continuing fires in the valley (to consume the refuse and dead bodies) apparently led the people to transfer the name to the place where the wicked dead suffer." This just is not the case.

In the Old Testament, the Israelites did burn sons in the fires as part of a sacrifice to false gods, but not for the purpose of punishment, or torture. By the time of the New Testament period, hundreds of years later, the only thing thrown in Gehenna was trash and the dead bodies of executed criminals. For what purpose were these thrown into Gehenna? It was used as an incinerator, a furnace for destroying things by burning them. Notice that any bodies thrown in Gehenna during the New Testament period were already dead. Thus, if anything, these people saw Gehenna as a place where they destroyed their trash and the bodies of dead criminals. Thus, if Jesus used this to illustrate the place of the wicked, it would have represented destruction as the punishment.

---

[10] Chad Brand et al., eds., "Gehenna," *Holman Illustrated Bible Dictionary* (Nashville, TN: Holman Bible Publishers, 2003), 632.

How Are We to Understand the "Fire"?

Mark 9:43-48 English Standard Version (ESV)

⁴³ And if your hand causes you to sin, cut it off. It is better for you to enter life crippled than with two hands to go to hell, to the unquenchable fire.⁴⁵ And if your foot causes you to sin, cut it off. It is better for you to enter life lame than with two feet to be thrown into hell. ⁴⁷ And if your eye causes you to sin, tear it out. It is better for you to enter the kingdom of God with one eye than with two eyes to be thrown into hell, ⁴⁸ 'where their worm does not die and the fire is not quenched.'

Matthew 13:42 English Standard Version (ESV)

⁴² and throw them into the fiery furnace. In that place there will be weeping and gnashing of teeth.

Here is why we should use the transliteration as opposed to the English "hell." Jesus did not use the word "Hades" in the above texts, the equivalent of Sheol, but rather Gehenna. Jesus used comparisons in his teaching, using things that his listeners could relate. As we learned in the above Gehenna was a garbage dump that was used as an incinerator, to destroy whatever was thrown in, and only the bodies of criminals were thrown in after they were already dead. In other words, the fire was used as a symbol, not of torment, but rather of being destroyed, complete destruction, namely annihilation by fire.

What did Jesus mean by "there will be weeping and gnashing of teeth"? We can look at what he said about those, who believed they were on the right path,

Matthew 7:21-23 English Standard Version (ESV)

²¹ "Not everyone who says to me, 'Lord, Lord,' will enter the kingdom of heaven, but the one who does the will of my Father who is in heaven. ²² On that day many will say to me, 'Lord, Lord, did we not prophesy in your name, and cast out demons in your name, and do many mighty works in your name?' ²³ And then will I declare to them, 'I never knew you; depart from me, you workers of lawlessness.'

In other words, those who will be weeping and gnashing of teeth" are those who believed they had the truth, but did not. Can we imagine giving our whole life to what we think to be the correct path, only to get to the edge and discover, we are on the wrong path because we chose to do our will, not the will of the Father? Now then, what about what John penned in the book of Revelation?

Revelation 21:8 English Standard Version (ESV)

⁸ But as for the cowardly, the faithless, the detestable, as for murderers, the sexually immoral, sorcerers, idolaters, and all liars, their portion will be in the lake that burns with fire and sulfur, which is the second death."

John speaks of a "lake that burns with fire and sulfur," where the wicked are thrown. It would seem that if hellfire were the truth, this would be the place. However, we are simply told by John; this is "the second death." Moreover, he had told his readers earlier,

Revelation 20:13-14 English Standard Version (ESV)

[13] And the sea gave up the dead who were in it, Death and Hades gave up the dead who were in them, and they were judged, each one of them, according to what they had done. [14] Then Death and Hades were thrown into the lake of fire. This is the second death, the lake of fire.

Notice that death, which is what we inherited from our first parents Adam and Eve, as well as Hades (gravedom), is going to be "thrown into the lake of fire." Is not death and Hades abstract, are they able to be tormented and suffer forever. No. However, the fire does picture their eternal destruction, which will take place once they 'give up the dead who were in them.' Note that Paul clearly said, "The last enemy to be destroyed is death." – 1 Corinthians 15:26.

The fire and burning within Scripture are simply representing annihilation or eternal destruction. Therefore, there is no eternal torment in Sheol (gravedom), Hades (the equivalent of Sheol) hell (English translation), Gehenna (symbol of destruction), or the lake of fire (symbol of destruction). What about the parable of the sheep (righteous) and the goats (wicked), which has the goats, or the wicked going away into eternal punishment?

Matthew 25:46 English Standard Version (ESV)

46 And there will go away into eternal punishment [*Kolasin*], but the righteous into eternal life."

Kolasin "akin to *kolazoo*"[11] "This means 'to cut short,' 'to lop,' 'to trim,' and figuratively a. 'to impede,' 'restrain,' and b. 'to punish,' and in the passive 'to suffer loss.'[12] The first part of the sentence is only in harmony with the second part of the sentence, if the eternal punishment is eternal death. The wicked receive eternal death and the righteous eternal life. We might at that Matthews Gospel was primarily for the Jewish Christians, and under the Mosaic Law, God would punish those who violated the law, saying they "shall be cut off [penalty of death] from Israel." (Ex 12:15; Lev 20:2-3) We need further to consider,

---

[11] W. E. Vine, Merrill F. Unger, and William White Jr., Vine's Complete Expository Dictionary of Old and New Testament Words (Nashville, TN: T. Nelson, 1996), 498.

[12] Gerhard Kittel, Gerhard Friedrich, and Geoffrey William Bromiley, Theological Dictionary of the New Testament (Grand Rapids, MI: W.B. Eerdmans, 1985), 451.

2 Thessalonians 1:8-9 English Standard Version (ESV)

⁸ in flaming fire, inflicting vengeance on those who do not know God and on those who do not obey the gospel of our Lord Jesus. ⁹ They will suffer the punishment of eternal destruction, away from the presence of the Lord and from the glory of his might

Notice that Paul says too that the punishment for the wicked is "eternal destruction." Many times in talking with those that support the position of eternal torment in some hellfire, they will add a word to Matthew 25:46 in their paraphrase of the verse, 'eternal conscious punishment.' However, Jesus does not tell us what the eternal punishment is, just that it is a punishment, and it is eternal. Therefore, those who support eternal conscious fiery torment will read the verse to mean just that, while those, who hold the position of eternal destruction, will take Matthew 25:46 to mean that. Considering that Jesus does not define what the eternal punishment is, this verse is not a proof text for either side of the argument. Does Jesus' parable, The Rich Man, and Lazarus, not support the hellfire doctrine? (Luke 16:19-31)

Interpreting Parables

Jesus gave us some 40 parables or illustrations, filling them with symbols and images that represented a message he was trying to share. Now, we get to this one, and we want to take it literally? Robert H. Stein writes,

> Similarly, the parable of the rich man and Lazarus (Luke 16:19–31) is to be interpreted as a parable, and thus according to the rules governing the interpretation of parables. It is not to be interpreted as a historical account. (Luke reveals this by the introduction "A certain man ..." which is used in the Gospel to introduce parables [cf. Luke 10:30; 14:16; 15:11; 16:1; 19:12]. This is clearer in the Greek text than in most translations, but it is fairly obvious in the NASB.)[13]

In discussing interpretation rules, stein goes on to say,

> In a similar way, there are different "game" rules involved in the interpretation of the different kinds of biblical literature. The author has played his "game," has sought to convey his meaning, under the rules covering the particular literary form he used. Unless we know those rules, we will almost certainly misinterpret his meaning. If we interpret a parable (Luke 16:19–31) as if it were narrative, or if we interpret poetry (Judg. 5) as if it were narrative, we will err. Similarly, if we interpret a narrative such as the resurrection of Jesus

---

[13] Robert H. Stein, A Basic Guide to Interpreting the Bible: Playing by the Rules (Grand Rapids, MI: Baker Books, 1994), 30.

(Matt. 28:1–10) as a parable, we will also err (1 Cor. 15:12–19).[14]

Step One in Understanding Parables

Read the context of the parable. You need to find out the setting of the parable, looking for the conditions and the circumstances. Why was the parable told? What prompted its being told?

Step Two in Understanding Parables

Consider the cultural backgrounds, such as the laws and customs of the setting, as well as the idioms that were spoken of earlier.

Step Three in Understanding Parables

This is a two-point step. The first point is to look to the author of the parable for the upcoming meaning of the parable. An interpreter of a parable by Jesus would see what he meant in the context it was spoken, and then consider his teaching as a whole. The second point is, do not assign subjective meanings to the elements of a parable. Generally, a parable teaches one basic point.

Stage One: Discovering the Main Characters

In any given parable, it is highly important to find the main 2–3 characters.

---

[14] IBID., 76.

Stage Two: Looking to the End

As is true with any kind of story, the end of the story carries the weight of importance. This is no different with parables. The ending is where the answers lie.

Stage Three: Who Carries the Conversation

Which character carries the conversation?

Stage Four: Who Gets the Most Press

Generally, whoever gets the most coverage in a story is the primary character, followed by the secondary person that must exist to facilitate the story and its main point.[15]

The setting of the parable of The rich man and Lazarus (Lu 16:19-31) is Jesus speaking, with the Pharisees listening in, who were well known as one who hungered for riches. What was Jesus teaching by this parable?

It had nothing to do with punishment for sin. It had to do with two different groups of people, the rich man (Jewish religious leaders) and the beggar Lazarus (poor Jewish people), as there was about to be a drastic change in their privileged and lowly positions. The Rich man, the Jewish religious leaders, opposed Jesus and the Good News of the

---

[15] Edward D. Andrews, A BASIC GUIDE TO BIBLICAL INTERPRETATION Understanding the Correct Methods of Interpretation (Christian Publishing House, Cambridge, OH, 2014), 313.

Kingdom that he brought because he was busy sharing it with the common Jewish people. This, in fact, tormented the Jewish religious leaders to no end, to the point of their seeking to kill him. (Luke 20:19, 20, 46, 47) Conversely, the beggar Lazarus represents, the poor, common Jewish people, who were looked upon with disdain, like beggars by the Jewish religious leaders, were being given the privilege position of becoming disciples of Jesus, and the first to enter into the kingdom.—1 Cor. 1:26-29.

What is the meaning of the "tormented with fire and sulfur" in Revelation 14:9-11?

Revelation 14:9-11 English Standard Version (ESV)

⁹ And another angel, a third, followed them, saying with a loud voice, "If anyone worships the beast and its image and receives a mark on his forehead or on his hand, ¹⁰ he also will drink the wine of God's wrath, poured full strength into the cup of his anger, and he will be tormented with fire and sulfur in the presence of the holy angels and in the presence of the Lamb. ¹¹ And the smoke of their torment goes up forever and ever, and they have no rest, day or night, these worshipers of the beast and its image, and whoever receives the mark of its name."

In the above text, those who worshipping the symbolic "beast and its image," they will be "tormented with fire and sulfur." The context here is not what happens after these one's deaths, but rather what happens to them while they are alive. What is it that torments these ones while they are alive? It is the proclamations of Christians that worshipers of the "beast and its image" will experience, to such a level that it is referred to as "tormented with fire and sulfur." Looking at the context of 14:11, it is not the torment that lasts forever; it is 'the smoke of their torment that goes up forever and ever.' What is smoke is a signal of their symbolic burning that will rise forever because the lesson learned will never be forgotten. Is there yet another example of this in Scripture? Yes.

The Judgment of Edom

Isaiah 34:9-12 English Standard Version (ESV)

9 And the streams of Edom shall be turned into pitch,
 and her soil into sulfur;
 her land shall become burning pitch.
10 Night and day it shall not be quenched;
its smoke shall go up forever.
From generation to generation it shall lie waste;
 none shall pass through it forever and ever.
11 But the hawk and the porcupine shall possess it,
 the owl and the raven shall dwell in it.
He shall stretch the line of confusion over it,
 and the plumb line of emptiness.
12 Its nobles—there is no one there to call it a kingdom,
 and all its princes shall be nothing.

Was Edom thrown into some literal hellfire to burn forever? No. The Edomite nation, an enemy of God's people, was removed, which is described in the above in poetic terms, highly symbolic language. It was as though fire and sulfur consumed Edom. If we were to go to the geographical location of ancient Edom, would we see smoke still rising? No. The smoke was and still is today, a signal of a lesson learned from the destruction that Edom faced. This smoke filled lesson will rise forever, in that the lesson learned will live on forever through the Word of God. After Jesus destroys the last enemy death, is it believed that the Bible will no longer be needed? The Bible is a book that will stand forever, as a signal of what humanity already experienced. Let us take this one step further as we look at our next text that is often drawn on to support hellfire doctrine.

Revelation 20:10 English Standard Version (ESV)

10 and the devil who had deceived them was thrown into the lake of fire and sulfur where the beast and the false prophet were, and they will be tormented (Greek, *basanos*) day and night forever and ever.

The Greek word used here for "torment," *basanizo*, primarily means "to test by rubbing on the touchstone" (basanos, "a touchstone"), then, "to question by applying torture."[16] The Bible is our case law (law established by previous verdicts), which will serve as a touchstone[17] (a standard by which something is judged) that humans were never designed to walk on their own, but to live under the sovereignty of their Creator. The issues raised by Satan will have been settled by humanities walking through thousands of years of an object lesson, for which the Bible is the case law, the touchstone, which will be around forever, as a reminder of the issues raised and settled.

The Moral Test

We know that man and woman were created in the image of God, and so when we hear of people who have tortured criminals, we call that inhumane. Would we expect that the One, whose image we are made in would see the eternal torment of sinners as humane? This would be incompatible with the very person of God. How are we to know how God views justice?

---

[16] W. E. Vine, Merrill F. Unger, and William White Jr., Vine's Complete Expository Dictionary of Old and New Testament Words (Nashville, TN: T. Nelson, 1996), 176.

[17] A touchstone is a hard black stone formerly used to test the purity of gold and silver according to the color of the streak left when the metal was rubbed against it.

(Exodus 21:23-24) But if there is harm, then you shall pay life for life, eye for eye, tooth for tooth, hand for hand, foot for foot,

(Leviticus 24:20) fracture for fracture, eye for eye, tooth for tooth; whatever injury he has given a person shall be given to him.

(Deuteronomy 19:21) Your eye shall not pity. It shall be life for life, eye for eye, tooth for tooth, hand for hand, foot for foot.

(Judges 1:7) And Adoni-bezek said, "Seventy kings with their thumbs and their big toes cut off used to pick up scraps under my table. As I have done, so God has repaid me." And they brought him to Jerusalem, and he died there.

(Matthew 5:38-42) "You have heard that it was said, 'An eye for an eye and a tooth for a tooth.' But I say to you, Do not resist the one who is evil. But if anyone slaps you on the right cheek, turn to him the other also. And if anyone would sue you and take your tunic, let him have your cloak as well. And if anyone forces you to go one mile, go with him two miles. Give to the one who begs from you, and do not refuse the one who would borrow from you."

The above texts are but a few of how God views justice, and it is all too clear that he sees it as the punishment needs to be proportionate, to be the best response to crime. In other words, if an Israelite were to steal his neighbor's cow, he would have to replace it with the cow, and any financial loss he suffered, even some extra as punitive damages. However, would God expect that thief to have to work as a slave to his neighbor for the rest of his life, and his children and grand children's lives as well? Note that that punishment would be way out of proportion to the crime.

Now, let us look at the punishment that God gave Adam and Eve if they were to rebel sinfully, rejecting him and his sovereignty, by choosing to eat from the tree he had commanded them not to eat from.

Genesis 2:17 English Standard Version (ESV)

17 but of the tree of the knowledge of good and evil you shall not eat, for in the day that you eat of it you shall surely die."

Eat from the tree (i.e., reject God as sovereign) = death. The punishment for sin was death. Please go back and look at Genesis 2:17 in the Bible, in several different translations. Do we notice some footnote from God that said, "And 4,000 years from now, when Jesus arrives, I am going to change the sentence from death to eternal torment in some literal lake of fire?"

Imagine we live in some small American town. We get our driver's licenses. Then, one day, we are pulled over for going 35-Miles Per Hour (MPH) in a 25 MPH zone. The police officer writes us a ticket and tells us to appear in court the following month, where the judge will fine us $50.00. We arrive at court the next month, and are in front of the magistrate, and he just found us guilty and sentences us not to a $50.00 fine, but to be taken outside of the courthouse and shot to death by a firing squad. Would anyone suggest that the punishment of a death sentence was proportionate to the crime of a speeding ticket? Would anyone find justice in the law enforcement officer saying the penalty was a mere $50.00 fine, and then the judge later raising the penalty to such an extreme level of capital punishment? God gave Adam the sentence of death, for committing the greatest sin of any human in history, as he had rejected God in perfection, and sentencing billions to death along with him. Would it then be justice, for God to raise the punishment bar to eternal torment in the Lake of Fire? Let us now look at imperfect humanity.

(Romans 3:23) for all have sinned and fall short of the glory of God,

(Romans 5:12) therefore, just as sin came into the world through one man, and death through sin, and so death spread to all men because all sinned

(Romans 6:7) For one who has died has been set free from sin.

(Romans 6:23) For the wages of sin is death, but the free gift of God is eternal life in Christ Jesus our Lord.

If Adam commits the greatest sin a human could commit, and he gets death, how is it justice that imperfect humans are supposedly getting eternal torment in a Lake of Fire?

There are five factors to imperfect humans being even less culpable (Guilty) than Adam was. **(1)** We are imperfect and live in an imperfect world, compounded by the fact that God's Word says we are mentally bent and lean toward doing bad. We read, "When the LORD saw that the wickedness of man on the earth was great and that the whole bent of his thinking was never anything but evil, the LORD regretted that he had ever made man on the earth." (Gen. 6:5, AT) **(2)** We have a wicked spirit creature, Satan the Devil, who is misleading the entire world of humankind. We read, "Be sober-minded; be watchful. Your adversary the devil prowls around like a roaring lion, seeking someone to devour." (1 Pet 5:8, ESV) **(3)** We live in a world that caters to the imperfect flesh. We read, "For all that is in the world, the desires of the flesh and the desires of the eyes and pride in possessions, is not from the Father but is from the world. And the world is passing away along with its desires, but whoever does the will of God abides forever." (1 John 2:16-17) **(4)** We are unable to understand our inner person, which the Bible informs us is wicked: "The heart is deceitful above all things and desperately sick; who can understand it?" (Jer. 17:9) **(5)** In imperfection, man is unable of directing his own step. – Jeremiah 10:23.

Unlike Adam, we are imperfect from the start, and Adam received death for sin. Adam was perfect, with the natural desire to do good, he was mentally perfect, and he lived in a paradise, in direct communication with God. We are born mentally bent toward sin. We have Satan and demons after us. Our natural desire is toward bad. We have an imperfect, fallen world that surrounds us, which caters to our flesh desires. We have a heart (i.e., inner person) that is deceitful and desperately sick and are unable to walk on our own. Thus, who can make the case that it is right, and just that imperfect humans are to receive eternal torment in some literal Lake of Fire? If one who dies, is freed from sin, by having paid the wages of sin, which was paid for through death (Rom 6:23), not the ransom of Christ, why should he then be liable so at to have to suffer eternally in some fiery torment?

If humanity were punishing another human being with deliberate torture of fire, we would find this to be sickening and abhorrent. Our finding it so sickening and abhorrent is actually based on the conscience that God gave man, that same man, who was made in the image of God. This same God clearly stated that such an idea would never have even come into his mind.

Jeremiah 7:31 English Standard Version (ESV)

³¹ And they have built the high places of Topheth, which is in the Valley of the Son of Hinnom, to burn their sons and their daughters in the fire, which I did not command, **nor did it come into my mind**.

CHAPTER 2 Is the Hellfire Doctrine Truly Just?

Genesis 1:27-28 English Standard Version (ESV)

27 So God created man in his own image, in the image of God he created him; male and female he created them.

28 And God blessed them. And God said to them, "Be fruitful and multiply and fill the earth and subdue it, and have dominion over the fish of the sea and over the birds of the heavens and over every living thing that moves on the earth."

It was God's intention that his first couple, namely, Adam and Eve were to procreate, and cultivate the Garden of Eden until it covered the entire earth, filled with humans worshipping him. – Genesis 1:28

If the first couple had not rebelled, they and their offspring could have lived forever.--Genesis 2:15-17

One of the angels in heaven (who became Satan), abused his free will (James 1:14-15). He then willfully chose to rebel against God. Satan used a lowly serpent to contribute to Adam and Eve abusing their free will, and disobeying God, believing they did not need him, and could walk on their own. – Genesis 3:1-6; Job 1-2.

God removed the rebellious Adam and Eve from the Garden of Eden. (Gen. 3:23-24) The first human couple had children, but they all grew old and eventually died. (Gen. 3:19; Rom. 5:12), just as the animals died. – Ecclesiastes 3:18-20

Genesis 6:5 (AT) tells us just before the flood of Noah, that "the wickedness of man on earth was great, and the whole bent of his thinking was never anything but evil." After the flood, God said of man, "the bent of man's mind may be evil from his very youth." (Gen 8:21, AT) Jeremiah 10:23 tells us "that it is not in man who walks to direct his steps." Jeremiah 17:9 tells us that "The heart is deceitful above all things, and desperately sick; who can understand it?" Yes, the man was not designed to walk on his own. However, the man was also not designed with absolute free will, but free will under the sovereignty of his Creator. The imperfect man is mentally bent toward wickedness, fleshly desires, to which Satan has set up this world, so it caters to the fallen flesh of imperfect humans. The apostle John tells us, "For all that is in the world, the desires of the flesh and the desires of the eyes and pride of life, is not from the Father but is from the world." – 1 John 2:16.

Getting back to Genesis 1:27 that says, "God created man in his own image, in the image of God he created him; male and female he created them," which means that man is born with a moral nature, which creates within him a conscience that reflects God's moral values. (Rom 2:14-15) It acts as a moral law within all imperfect humans but even more so, those who have trained the conscience with God's Word. However, it has an opponent as fallen man also possesses the "law of sin," 'missing the mark of perfection,' the natural desire toward wickedness. Listen to the internal battle of the apostle Paul. – Romans 6:12; 7:22-23.

Romans 7:21-24 English Standard Version (ESV)

21 So I find it to be a law that when I want to do right, evil lies close at hand. 22 For I delight in the law of God, in my inner being, 23 but I see in my members another law waging war against the law of my mind and making me captive to the law of sin that dwells in my members. 24 Wretched man that I am! Who will deliver me from this body of death?

However, there is hope,

Romans 7:25 English Standard Version (ESV)

25 Thanks be to God through Jesus Christ our Lord! So then, I myself serve the law of God with my mind, but with my flesh I serve the law of sin.

Yes, even imperfect man and woman have a conscience that reflects God's moral values. Therefore, when we hear of such things as ones being tortured, it is repugnant to us. Even if the person has committed some heinous crime, it is still sickening and abhorrent to the human mind, which reflects God's moral values on a small scale in our human imperfection. Therefore, we can only wonder how God, who has perfect moral values, would view the idea of torturing humans for an eternity, which is what the hellfire doctrine teaches.

Jeremiah 7:31 English Standard Version (ESV)

³¹ And they have built the high places of Topheth, which is in the Valley of the Son of Hinnom, to burn their sons and their daughters in the fire, which I did not command, nor did it come into my mind.

Imagine if we can, we have come home to find that our husband has inserted a pipe up the rectum of our 17-year-old daughter, with it coming out her mouth. He has her over a fire and is slowly cooking her alive. He has the fire set, so it will burn her very slowly, lasting days. He says that he is tired of her sinful actions, and she must pay for her rebellious spirit. How would our Christian conscience take that scene, would we simply set our purse down, and start helping him turn her on the thin rod on which she is impaled for roasting over the fire? Would we have no feeling as she screams out in agony? How do we place a loving and just God in such a light, when we only have a fraction of his moral values, and know that this scene would be so shocking and hurtful, it is unthinkable. Likely, as the reader started this paragraph, the language of even saying such things was so revolting that we have questioned why we even bought such a book. Keep in mind, it is our God given conscience that made us feel that way.

Regardless of this hypothetical daughter's sinful nature, and her rebellious spirit, a parent's heart would be torn in two. The disdain for the husband, the one who applied the torture, would be unbearable. The love of God is merciful and has the feeling of sympathy. A loving father may choose to punish his child but never torture. In fact, the United States will not allow any form of capital punishment (i.e., death penalty) that includes any pain and suffering. This is true, even when they are executing people for the vilest crimes.

Nevertheless, much of Christianity teaches that God is a torturer, and his form of justice is to exceed the crime, because he is vindictive, as a human rejected his sovereignty, so he burns this one alive, in an eternal hellfire. If a child refused to follow the rules of the house, would we kick her out, or would we burn her slowly over a fiery pit in the backyard? Which is more just, to kick a person out of eternal life (annihilationism), or to torturously burn them alive for an eternity. Who would create a torture chamber, and see that as justice? Would this be one who is repeatedly described as the epitome of love, justice, mercy, kindness, and wisdom?

1 John 4:8 English Standard Version (ESV)

[8] Anyone who does not love does not know God, because God is love.

Unreasonable Doctrine?

Does the above almighty being inflict eternal torture on a person, who has only sinned for 70 years? Does this sound like a person that deserves to be loved? Did not Adolf Hitler do the same thing to the Jews and Christians? Even if a human sinned every day of an 80-year lifetime grievously, would eternal fiery torment be a just punishment? Hardly! It would be unjust to God, who already told us how to view justice when he said an eye for an eye, a life for a life.

Deuteronomy 32:4 English Standard Version (ESV)

⁴ "The Rock, his work is perfect,

for all his ways are justice.

A God of faithfulness and without iniquity,

just and upright is he.

What Does Deuteronomy 32:4 Mean?

God's justice, like every other aspect of his unparalleled personality, is perfect, not lacking in anything. Every time God expresses his justice, it is flawless, never too lenient and never too harsh.

Holman Old Testament Commentary

32:1-4. Although the words of Moses in his song were designed to testify against Israel's coming defections, the true subject of the song was the greatness of our God. Once convicted of their sin, Israel would be brought back to God not by the failure of their idols but by the supreme faithfulness and beauty of the Rock of Israel, a God who does no wrong.[18]

New American Commentary

32:3–4 There clearly is a subject shift in v. 3, where Moses appears as a character witness on the Lord's behalf. Also addressing the heavens and the earth, he extols the Lord's greatness, especially by the public proclamation of his name, that is, of his reputation (v. 3; cf. Exod 33:19; 34:5–6). The expected result was that all who heard should ascribe greatness ("praise") to God. Knowledge of God can lead to no other response than to acknowledge his might. Specific expressions of his power are his identification as "the Rock" (haṣṣûr; cf. vv. 15, 18, 30; Hab 1:12), the foundation and fortress (cf. Pss 31:3; 62:7; 71:3; 89:26; 95:1; Isa 30:29) whose works are upright (thus tā mîm, "having integrity") and whose ways are characterized by justice (mišpāṭ, "rectitude"; cf. Gen 18:25; Job 40:8; Pss 111:7; 119:149). In the context of self-defense these attributes

---

[18] Anders, Max; McIntosh, Doug, *Deuteronomy*, Holman Old Testament Commentary (Nashville: Broadman & Holman Publishers, 2002), 359-360.

speak most particularly to the Lord's own character. Thus he is also faithful in the sense that he is dependable ('ĕmûnâ; cf. Pss 88:11; 89:2–3, 6, 9; Isa 25:1; Hos 2:19), devoid of any hint of injustice ('ên 'āwel), a God who is righteous and just in all he does (v. 4b). These descriptions are especially apropos in a legal setting in which the reputation of the Lord may be under attack as he himself proceeds to level charges of impropriety against his covenant partner Israel.[19]

The main thoughts here, which apply to our discussion is, "God does no wrong," a God "devoid of any hint of injustice ('ên 'āwel), a God, who is righteous and just in all he does (v. 4b)."

Tsadaq, "to be righteous, be in the right, be justified, be just." This verb, which occurs fewer than 40 times in biblical Hebrew, is derived from the noun tsedeq. The basic meaning of tsadaq is "to be righteous." It is a legal term which involves the whole process of justice. God "is righteous" in all of His relations ..."[20]

---

[19] Eugene H. Merrill, *Deuteronomy*, vol. 4, The New American Commentary (Nashville: Broadman & Holman Publishers, 1994), 410.

[20] W. E. Vine, Merrill F. Unger, and William White Jr., *Vine's Complete Expository Dictionary of Old and New Testament Words* (Nashville, TN: T. Nelson, 1996), 205.

Now, let us look at the Son of God, and his perception of retribution.

Matthew 5:38-42 English Standard Version (ESV)

³⁸ "You have heard that it was said, 'An eye for an eye and a tooth for a tooth.'³⁹ But I say to you, Do not resist the one who is evil. But if anyone slaps you on the right cheek, turn to him the other also. ⁴⁰ And if anyone would sue you and take your tunic, let him have your cloak as well. ⁴¹ And if anyone forces you to go one mile, go with him two miles. ⁴² Give to the one who begs from you, and do not refuse the one who would borrow from you.

What Did Jesus Mean?

Holman New Testament Commentary

5:38–42. As many people do today, the scribes and Pharisees of Jesus' day must have taken the "eye for an eye" passages (Exod. 21:24; Lev. 24:19–20; Deut. 19:21) as justification for hurting others at least as badly as they had been hurt. The law was not given to exact revenge, but to legislate justice. Breaking the law has consequences, but personal vengeance has no place. These passages have often been wrongly taken as a minimum guideline for retaliation. What Jesus clarifies is that they were always intended as a maximum or a ceiling for retaliation, and that mercy was always an acceptable intention underlying these laws.

For the kingdom servant, legalistically "letting the punishment fit the crime" and insisting upon a "pound of flesh" falls short. We must actually consider blessing the repentant criminal. Mercy (withholding deserved punishment) and grace (giving undeserved gifts) are legitimate norms of conduct.

The **one mile** (5:41) refers to the practice of the Roman soldiers requiring civilians to carry their burden for one mile. By Roman law, the soldier could require no more than one mile of a single porter, but Jesus' kingdom servants (in representing the gracious spirit of their king) are to go beyond what is required of them.[21]

New American Commentary

5:38–42 Jesus next alludes to Exod 21:24 and Deut. 19:21. Again, he formally abrogates an Old Testament command in order to intensify and internalize its application. This law originally prohibited the formal exaction of an overly severe punishment that did not fit a crime as well as informal, self-appointed

---

[21] Stuart K. Weber, *Matthew*, vol. 1, Holman New Testament Commentary (Nashville, TN: Broadman & Holman Publishers, 2000), 69.

vigilante action. Now Jesus teaches the principle that Christian kindness should transcend even straightforward tit-for-tat retribution. None of the commands of vv. 39–42 can easily be considered absolute; all must be read against the historical background of first-century Judaism. Nevertheless, in light of prevailing ethical thought Jesus contrasts radically with most others of his day in stressing the need to decisively break the natural chain of evil action and reaction that characterizes human relationships.

Antistēnai ("resist") in v. 39 was often used in a legal context (cf. Isa 50:8) and in light of v. 40 is probably to be taken that way here. Jesus' teaching then parallels 1 Cor 6:7 against not taking fellow believers to court, though it could be translated somewhat more broadly as "do not take revenge on someone who wrongs you" (GNB). We must nevertheless definitely resist evil in certain contexts (cf. Jas 4:7; 1 Pet 5:9). Striking a person on the right cheek suggests a backhanded slap from a typically right-handed aggressor and was a characteristic Jewish form of insult. Jesus tells us not to trade such insults even if it means receiving more. In no sense does v. 39 require Christians to subject themselves or others to physical danger or abuse, nor does it bear directly on the pacifism-just war debate. Verse 40 is clearly limited to a legal context. One must be willing to give as collateral an outer garment—more than what the law could require, which was merely an inner garment (cf. Exod 22:26–27). *Coat* and *shirt* reflect contemporary parallels to "cloak" and "tunic," though both of the latter looked more like long robes. Verse 41 continues the legal motif by referring to Roman conscription of private citizens to help carry military equipment for soldiers as they traveled.

Each of these commands requires Jesus' followers to act more generously than what the letter of the law demanded. "Going the extra mile" has rightly become a proverbial expression and captures the essence of all of Jesus' illustrations. Not only must disciples reject all behavior motivated only by a desire for retaliation, but they also must positively work for the good of those with whom they would otherwise be at odds. In v. 42 Jesus calls his followers to give to those who ask and not turn from those who would borrow. He presumes that the needs are genuine and commands us not to ignore them, but he does not specifically mandate how best we can help. As Augustine rightly noted, the text says "give to everyone that asks," not "give everything to him that asks" (*De Sermone Domine en Monte* 67). Compare Jesus' response to the request made of him in Luke 12:13–15. It is also crucial to note that "a willingness to forego one's personal rights, and to allow oneself to be insulted and imposed upon, is not incompatible with a firm stand for matters of principle and for the rights of others (cf. Paul's attitude in Acts 16:37; 22:25; 25:8–12)." Verses 39–42 thus comprise a "focal instance" of nonretaliation; specific, extreme commands attract our attention to a key ethical theme that must be variously applied as circumstances change.[22]

If the above are examples of how the Father and the Son see justice, retaliation, and retribution, it would clearly be injustice to torment someone in a pit of fire eternally, for a limited number of sins that was committed over a 70-80 year period.

There is only one person, who knows what happens after death, and it is God. He made it all too clear as to what happens to humans at death.

Ecclesiastes 3:19-20 English Standard Version (ESV)

[19] For what happens to the children of man and what happens to the beasts is the same; as one dies, so dies the other. They all have the same breath, and man has no advantage over the beasts, for all is vanity. [20] All go to one place. All are from the dust, and to dust all return.

---

[22] Craig Blomberg, *Matthew*, vol. 22, The New American Commentary (Nashville: Broadman & Holman Publishers, 1992), 113–114.

These verses have no mention of some eternal fiery torment. Humans simply return to the dust from which they came, no longer in existence, when they die. Some will receive a resurrection from the dead, other will simply remain dead forever.

If a person is to feel the torment of eternal hellfire, they have to be conscious. However, God inspired Solomon to write, "Yes, the living know they are going to die, but the dead know nothing. They have no further reward; they are completely forgotten." (Eccles 9:5) Based on this, it is impossible for those that have died, who "know nothing," to have knowledge of the anguishes of hellfire.

Dangerous Doctrine?

Some Christians would actually make the statement that 'the doctrine of hellfire is useful.' Why would they say that? They believe that it helps deter the Christian from sinning. Well, the same thing is believed about the death penalty for capital murder. Are not the United States prisons filled with death row inmates? In fact, the prison system is filled with all kinds of Christians, committing any number of different crimes. The truth is, the hellfire doctrine is actually harmful. If a person accepts that God tortures people for eternity, for sinning a mere 70-80 years, will they not view humans torturing humans as acceptable. Did not the Catholic Church torture Christians during the Inquisitions for simply disobeying the church? Yes, they burned them at the stake, stretched them on a rack,[23] until their bones broke, and beat them relentlessly.

If hellfire is so unreasonable logically, why do so many Christians, who claim to have the mind of Christ, accept such cruelty from their loving God? "Mind control (also known as brainwashing, coercive persuasion, thought control, or thought reform) is an indoctrination process that results in

---

[23] The rack is a torture device consisting of a rectangular, usually wooden frame, slightly raised from the ground, with a roller at one or both ends. The victim's ankles are fastened to one roller and the wrists are chained to the other. As the interrogation progresses, a handle and ratchet attached to the top roller are used to very gradually stepwise increase the tension on the chains, inducing excruciating pain. By means of pulleys and levers this roller could be rotated on its own axis, thus straining the ropes until the sufferer's joints were dislocated and eventually separated. Additionally, if muscle fibres are stretched excessively, they lose their ability to contract, rendering them ineffective.

One gruesome aspect of being stretched too far on the rack is the loud popping noises made by snapping cartilage, ligaments or bones. One powerful method for putting pressure upon prisoners was to force them to watch someone else being subjected to the rack. Confining the prisoner on the rack enabled further tortures to be simultaneously applied, typically including burning the flanks with hot torches or candles or using pincers made with specially roughened grips to tear out the nails of the fingers and toes.--http://en.wikipedia.org/wiki/Rack_(torture)

"an impairment of autonomy, an inability to think independently, and a disruption of beliefs and affiliations. In this context, brainwashing refers to the involuntary reeducation of basic beliefs and values"[24] The term has been applied to any tactic, psychological or otherwise, which can be seen as subverting an individual's sense of control over their own thinking, behavior, emotions or decision making."[25] Yes, these ones were raised in ultra-religious households, where they were taught the hellfire doctrine from childhood, up unto their adult years, so it is a deeply ingrain belief.

Keep in mind that after Adam sinned. Imperfect humans had and have had a natural inclination toward sin. It bears repeating again, Genesis 6:5 (AT) tells us just before the flood of Noah, that "the wickedness of man on earth was great, and the whole bent of his thinking was never anything but evil." After the flood, God said of man, "the bent of man's mind may be evil from his very youth." (Gen 8:21, AT) Jeremiah 10:23 tells us "that it is not in man who walks to direct his steps." Jeremiah 17:9 tells us that "The heart is deceitful above all things, and desperately sick; who can understand it?" Yes, man naturally leans toward bad.

---

[24] Kowal, D. M. (2000). Brainwashing. In A. E. Kazdin (Ed.) , Encyclopedia of psychology, Vol. 1 (pp. 463-464). American Psychological Association.

[25]

http://en.wikipedia.org/wiki/Brain_washing#cite_note-1

What is the Punishment for Sin?

If the hellfire doctrine does not exist, what is the punishment for sin? What is Adam's punishment for rejecting God, what is the rest of humanities punishment for rejecting the Gospel? What was Adam told would happen, if he sinned? He was told, "for in the day that you eat of it the tree of knowledge] you shall surely die." (Gen 2:17) What happened to Adam? God told him, "By the sweat of your face you shall eat bread, till you return to the ground, for out of it you were taken; for you are dust, and to dust you shall return." (Gen. 3:19) What did Paul say was the punishment for sin? "The wages of sin is death." (Rom. 6:23) Life was and is a gift from God. If we reject God, if we willfully, sin unrepentantly, the gift is taken away, and we die.

The same Christians who have been programmed to accept the contradiction of a loving God, who tortures humans forever, would actually ask, 'how is that just, because everyone dies?' It is true that we all die. Why? Paul tells us, "sin came into the world through one man [Adam], and death through sin, and so death spread to all men because all sinned." We are all sinners.

If we all are sinners, and we all die, what is the point in trying to live a Christlike life? Is it true justice, if the one who is attempting to live a virtuous life, should die, just as the wicked man dies? However, this is irrational thinking, and some things are being left out of the formula of justice.

While both die, the righteous one will receive a resurrection, with the hope of eternal life. We see that Jesus 'gave his life as a ransom for many' (Matt. 20:28). We see that "all who are in the tombs will hear [the] voice [of Jesus] and come out, those who have done good to the resurrection of life, and those who have done evil to the resurrection of judgment." (John 5:28-29) We are told, "that there is going to be a resurrection, both of the righteous and the unrighteous." – Acts 24:15

Romans 5:18-21 English Standard Version (ESV)

[18] Therefore, as one trespass led to condemnation for all men, so one act of righteousness leads to justification and life for all men. [19] For as by the one man's disobedience the many were made sinners, so by the one man's obedience the many will be made righteous. [20] Now the law came in to increase the trespass, but where sin increased, grace abounded all the more, [21] so that, as sin reigned in death, grace also might reign through righteousness leading to eternal life through Jesus Christ our Lord.

Righteous Receive the Resurrection of Life

The wages of sin is death, and wages of willful unrepentant sin is eternal death (Heb. 6:4-6; 10:26-31), never being resurrected, as Paul said, "will suffer the punishment of eternal destruction." (2 Thess. 1:9) It is true that when we die, we no longer exist, except in the memory of God, as dead is dead. However, as we are seeing here, the righteous will receive a resurrection. Even those in the Old Testament had a hope for something better, as Job's words clearly demonstrate,

Job 14:13-15 English Standard Version (ESV)

¹³ Oh that you would hide me in Sheol,

that you would conceal me until your wrath be past,

that you would appoint me a set time, and remember me!

¹⁴ **If a man dies, shall he live again?**

All the days of my service I would wait,

till my renewal should come.

¹⁵ **You would call, and I would answer you;**

you would long for the work of your hands.²⁶

The righteous man Job believed that his remaining faithful to God, would result in God remember him after he had died, and one day, he would be resurrected. Jesus himself, speaking to a Jewish audience, confirmed the hope that the Israelites had been carrying for 2,000 years,

---

²⁶ This led him to consider the doctrine of resurrection and to wonder if it would be best for him to die and thus rest until the day when the dead rise (14:13–17). – David S. Dockery et al., *Holman Bible Handbook* (Nashville, TN: Holman Bible Publishers, 1992), 316.

John 5:28-29 English Standard Version (ESV)

[28] Do not marvel at this, for an hour is coming when all who are in the tombs will hear his voice [29] and come out, those who have done good to the resurrection of life, and those who have done evil to the resurrection of judgment.

When Jesus returns, he will bring many angels, and wipe out the wicked. However, the righteous will not be destroyed, and the righteous prior to Jesus first coming back in the first century, will receive a resurrection. The unrighteous, which had never had the opportunity to know God, will also be resurrected for a chance to hear the Good News, and then, they will be judged on what they do during the millennial reign of Christ. Acts 24:15) Therefore, the punishment for sin is death, the punishment for those, who "keep on sinning deliberately after receiving the knowledge of the truth, there no longer remains a sacrifice for sins," i.e., eternal death. However, "there will be a resurrection of both the just and the unjust [i.e., those who never heard the Good News]." – Acts 24:15

Life on Earth under God's Kingdom

Isaiah 65:21-23 Updated American Standard Version (UASV)

[21] They shall build houses and inhabit them;
   they shall plant vineyards and eat their fruit.
[22] They shall not build and another inhabit;
   they shall not plant and another eat;

for like the days of a tree will the days of my people be,

   and the work of their hands my chosen ones will enjoy to the full.
23 They shall not labor in vain
   or bear children for calamity,
for they are the seed[27] made up of those blessed by Jehovah,,
   and their descendants with them.

On this, the Holman Old Testament Commentary says, "The injustices of life would disappear. Long life would be the rule for God's people, death at a hundred being like an infant's death that could only be explained as the death of a sinner. All of God's people would live to a ripe old age and enjoy the fruits of their life. The age of Messiah would clearly have dawned (cp. 11:6–9). No longer would people lose their property and crops to foreign invaders. Each of God's faithful people would enjoy the works of their hands. Labor would be rewarded in the field and in the birth place. Every newborn would escape the "horror of sudden disaster" (author's translation; NIV, misfortune). Curses would disappear. Every generation would be blessed by God."[28]

---

[27] I.e., *offspring*

[28] Anders, Max; Butler, Trent (2002-04-01). Holman Old Testament Commentary - Isaiah (p. 374). B&H Publishing. Kindle Edition.

Revelation 21:3-4 Updated American Standard Version (UASV)

3 And I heard a loud voice from the throne, saying, "Behold, the tabernacle of God is among men, and he will dwell[29] among them, and they shall be his people,[30] and God himself will be among them,[31] 4 and he will wipe away every tear from their eyes, and death shall be no more, neither shall there be mourning, nor crying, nor pain anymore, for the former things, have passed away."

"[God] will wipe away every tear from their eyes." (21:4) These are not tears of joy but rather tears that were the result of pain, suffering, old age, the loss of loved ones, and death. The Father will not only wipe away these tears of sorrow from our eyes but, he will remove them permanently forever, as he will have removed all that would ever lead to such tears, i.e., the removal of the *causes*.

"Death shall be no more." (21:4) Certainly, the enemy death has brought about more unwanted tears than anything else. After the thousand year reign of Christ, Satan will be released from the abyss for a while, succeeding to mislead many more. After that, those who have remained faithful will have the grip of death removed forever. The Father will

---

[29] Lit *he will tabernacle*

[30] Some mss *peoples*

[31] One early ms and be *their God*

remove the real cause of death; that is, the inherited sin from Adam. (Rom. 5:12) "The last enemy that will be abolished is death." (1 Cor. 15:26) Those who were faithful through the Great Tribulation, Armageddon, the Millennium, and the release of Satan for a little while will live for an eternity in a paradise earth, in human perfection, just as God had originally intended.

"Neither shall there be ... pain anymore." (21:4) The type of pain that is spoken of being removed here is the physical, mental, and emotional, which was brought on by the sin of Adam and the inherited imperfection that resulted after that. It will be no more.

This new life without tears, pain, mourning, crying, and death will certainly be a reality for those with a heavenly hope as they rule with Christ in heaven but also for those with an earthly hope, which is who is being spoken of here specifically. Notice that all of this was introduced with the words **"the tabernacle of God is among men."** (21:3) We know that men live here on earth. Moreover, the context is describing the renewed earth where **"death shall be no more."** This is referring the world where death had existed but will now be no more. Death has never existed in the spiritual heavens where the Father, the Son and the Holy Spirit, as well as the angels, live. However, for over six thousand years, death has existed here on the earth. Thus, the promises of Revelation 21:3-4 are meant specifically for those here on earth, which will be a restored or renewed earth.

The restored or renewed earth will be filled with people who fear God and sincerely love their neighbor. (Heb. 2:5; Lu 10:25-28.) The changes that take place as a result of God's heavenly Kingdom, namely, Jesus and his co-rulers, will be so weighty that the Bible speaks of "a new earth," i.e., a new faithful human society.

How is it that God "will dwell among them," that is among humankind after Armageddon? God would turn his attention to his people in the forthcoming renewed or restored earth, setting them free from sin and death. Then God will turn his attention to Satan the Devil, the god of this wicked world. The God of peace will abyss Satan for a thousand years, and then he will crush Satan by throwing him into the lake of fire. (2 Cor. 4:4; Rom. 16:20; Rev. 20:10, 14) After all of this, Jesus will hand the kingdom back over to the Father. (1 Cor. 15:28) After that, we do not know. However, we do know that more books will be opened during the millennium, where we will likely learn more.

CHAPTER 3 Is Hellfire Part of Divine Justice?

Genesis 1:27 tells us, "God created man in his own image, in the image of God he created him; male and female he created them." What does this verse mean? It means that man is born with a moral nature, which creates within him a conscience that reflects God's moral values. (Rom 2:14-15) It acts as a moral law within. Even in imperfection, we are born with a measure of that conscience, which can be developed toward good or bad. The Word of God develops a Christian conscience.

Shortly after 9 a.m. on an otherwise unassuming day in Newton, Conn., a gunman entered a kindergarten classroom at Sandy Hook Elementary School, beginning a rampage that has reportedly left as many as 27 people dead, 18 of whom are children.

When we think of the pain and suffering in this world, it troubles our inner person to no end. When we hear of a young twelve-year-old girl, who is harassed to the point that she climbs a sixty-foot tower, to jump to her death, we can barely control our wrath. When we think of an older woman in her seventies, beat to death by a young punk, who steals her purse, we wish we could have five minutes alone with him. When we think of the starvation, the genocides by dictators, the natural disaster, and the like, we are emotionally sickened. Why are we emotionally sickened? Because were created in the image of God, and we possess his moral values.

Have we taken the time to ponder what we are claiming about the hellfire doctrine? We are saying that a person born,

(1) Imperfect

(2) With human weaknesses

(3) Who are mentally bent toward evil

(4) Who have a treacherous heart (inner person), and are unable to know it

(5) Who were born a sinner through no fault of their own

(6) Who have a natural (although contrary to what God intended) desire to do bad

(7) Who naturally lean toward evil

(8) Who have only sinned for 70-80-years

These ones will be tormented with fire for eternity. This is sickening and abhorrent. Some do not even want the United States government to torture known terrorists. They say that makes us like them, we should take the moral high ground. Yet, we are to accept that **eternal** torture inflicted by God is somehow acceptable. If a person kept breaking city laws like stealing, and he just would not change, could he be tortured. Could we strap him to a table and beat him hour after hour, day after day, week after week, year after year?

What happens is that we will eventually feel sorry for this person, especially if the punishment does not fit the crime. Would we give a person who stole some candy a hundred years in a maximum-security prison? What should we think of a person that has meted out such a punishment? Would any of us as a loving parent burn our child with a lighter, thinking that was just punishment. Of course we would not, but we expect far worse out of God. Is that not contrary to Scripture? Is that not contrary to our sense of justice, which in turn is contrary to the Creator, in whose image in which we were created? When we set aside our church tradition for a moment and truly ponder Scripture and reason, things become clearer.

Irrational Teaching

1 John 4:8 English Standard Version (ESV)

[8] Anyone who does not love does not know God, because God is love.

Does this Scripture and the hundreds upon hundreds of other corresponding ones support God torturing someone, whose heart is treacherous, desires are toward evil, and natural leaning are toward sin, for a mere 80 years, forever. Bible scholars, pastors, and elders would have us think that this is divine justice. If this all is biblically true, this means that God planned or chose the world that would have a hellfire of torment, which would torture sinners for eternity. This does not sound like the God of the Bible, as far as this author is concerned. It would mean that God was responsible for torturing sinners for eternity.

God is the only person who knows what happens to us at death.[32] He has revealed this to use through the Scriptures. God had warned Adam, if he ate of the tree of knowledge of good and bad, if you eat of it you will surely die. (Gen. 2:17) Wise King Solomon wrote,

---

[32] WHERE ARE THE DEAD? Basic Bible Doctrines of the Christian Faith by Edward D. Andrews (See christianpublishers.org)

http://www.christianpublishers.org/apps/webstore/products/show/5341545

Ecclesiastes 3:19-20 English Standard Version (ESV)

¹⁹ For what happens to the children of man and what happens to the beasts is the same; as one dies, so dies the other. They all have the same breath, and man has no advantage over the beasts, for all is vanity.²⁰ All go to one place. All are from the dust, and to dust all return.

There is no mention of some eternal fiery torment. Think about this, God tells Adam, "of the tree of the knowledge of good and evil you shall not eat, for in the day that you eat of it you shall surely die." (Gen. 2:17) Why would God withhold the punishment of eternal torment from Adam and Eve? If hellfire were real, this would have been a very underhanded thing. Just think, he tells the people of the Old Testament that if you sin, "you shall surely die." Then, some 4,000 years later, he throws in, "oh, by the way, you will also burn in a fiery pit forever." Imagine that you broke a rule in school that you knew would get you detention. You arrive at detention after school, and the principal tells you, "Oh, by the way, we are going to beat you to death with a baseball bat."

Bad Bible Doctrine

The preaching of hellfire has been used as a scare tactic, which is a dreadful fear of God, not the biblical reverential fear of displeasing him. Psalm 111:10 says, "The fear of the Lord is the beginning of wisdom." We just saw God is love, why would it be prudent to fear him, and why would he want someone to fear him? Here is the answer from Norman L. Geisler,[33]

PROBLEM: John affirms here that "perfect love casts out all fear." Yet we are told that the "fear of the Lord is the beginning of knowledge" (Prov. 1:7) and that we should "serve the Lord with fear" (Ps. 2:11). Indeed, Paul said, "knowing ... the terror [fear] of the Lord, we persuade men" (2 Cor. 5:11).

SOLUTION: Fear is being used in different senses. Fear in the good sense is a reverential trust in God. In the bad sense it is a sense of recoiling torment in the face of God. While proper fear brings a healthy respect for God, unwholesome fear engenders an unhealthy sense that He is out to get us. Perfect love casts out this kind of "torment." When one properly understands that "God is love" (1 John 4:16), he can no longer fear Him in this unhealthy sense. For "he who fears has not been made perfect in love" (1 John 4:18). Nonetheless, at no time does proper love for God ever show disrespect for Him. Rather, it is perfectly compatible with a

---

[33] It should be noted that Dr. Norman L. Geisler does believe in the hellfire doctrine, and this author disagrees with him.

reverential awe for Him, which is what the Bible means by "fearing God" in the good sense (cf. 2 Cor. 7:1; 1 Peter 2:17).[34]

Again, religious leaders would be in denial to say that almost all scholars, pastors, and elders have not used hellfire, to scare people into becoming a disciple and keeping them. This is what the religious leaders do. When we go to the Bible belt part of the United States, do we find a lower crime or divorce rate? No, we do not. Another aspect to keep in mind, Christians that are fire and brimstone to the core, tend to be far more aggressive in their physical punishment of their children. Those who have a cruel God will tend to adopt that mindset with their children as well. The very heart and mind that God gave us are repelled by such a doctrine and the Bible itself says, When a person dies, "his breath departs, he returns to the earth; on that very day his plans perish.." – Psalm 146:4.

What Is the Punishment for Sin?

Genesis 2:17 English Standard Version (ESV)

[17] but of the tree of the knowledge of good and evil you shall not eat, for in the day that you eat of it you shall surely die."

---

[34] Thomas Howe; Norman L. Geisler. The Big Book of Bible Difficulties: Clear and Concise Answers from Genesis to Revelation (Kindle Locations 6287-6293). Kindle Edition.

Ezekiel 18:4 English Standard Version (ESV)

4 Behold, all souls are mine; the soul of the father as well as the soul of the son is mine: the soul who sins shall die.

Romans 6:23 English Standard Version (ESV)

23 For the wages of sin is death, but the free gift of God is eternal life in Christ Jesus our Lord.

Romans 5:12 English Standard Version (ESV)

12 Therefore, just as sin came into the world through one man, and death through sin, and so death spread to all men because all sinned

The penalty of death can be avoided, if we walk with God until our death, or Jesus return, whichever comes first.

Romans 12:2 English Standard Version (ESV)

2 Do not be conformed to this world, but be transformed by the renewal of your mind, that by testing you may discern what is the will of God, what is good and acceptable and perfect.

Good for Doing Good

Job 14:13-15 English Standard Version (ESV)

13 Oh that you would hide me in Sheol,
    that you would conceal me until your wrath be past,
    that you would appoint me a set time, and remember me!

¹⁴ If a man dies, shall he live again?
   All the days of my service I would wait,
   till my renewal should come.
¹⁵ You would call, and I would answer you;
   you would long for the work of your hands.

Yes, there us a resurrection hope, which will be covered in Chapter 3.

John 5:28-29 English Standard Version (ESV)

²⁸ Do not marvel at this, for an hour is coming when all who are in the tombs will hear his voice ²⁹ and come out, those who have done good to the resurrection of life, and those who have done evil to the resurrection of judgment.

The *College Press NIV Commentary* offers this thought, "In fact the time is coming when the dead will hear the voice of God and those who hear will live. Surely this implies a resurrection. Jesus expresses it stronger in verses 28f when he says that all in the graves will hear his voice, and they that hear will be raised to life. Two views of the resurrection jostle one another here: (1) as in the case of Lazarus (11:43) Jesus can summon the dead and give them physical life (2) the word of Jesus can give spiritual life to these who are dead in sin. Too much should not be made in the distinction of the two views because both are true and both are needed."[35]

[35] Beauford H. Bryant and Mark S. Krause, *John*, The College Press NIV Commentary (Joplin, MO: College Press Pub. Co., 1998), Jn 5:28–29.

CHAPTER 4 What Did Jesus Teach About Hell?

Mark 9:47-48 English Standard Version (ESV)	**Mark 9:47-48** Good News Translation (GNT)
[47] And if your eye causes you to sin, tear it out. It is better for you to enter the kingdom of God with one eye than with two eyes to be thrown into hell, [48] 'where their worm does not die and the fire is not quenched.'	[47] And if your eye makes you lose your faith, take it out! It is better for you to enter the Kingdom of God with only one eye than to keep both eyes and be thrown into hell. [48] There 'the worms that eat them never die, and the fire that burns them is never put out.'

Mark 9:47-48 Updated American Standard Version (UASV)

[47] And if your eye makes you stumble, throw it out, it is better for you to enter the kingdom of God with one eye, than, having two eyes, to be cast into Gehenna,[36] [48] where their worm does not die and the fire is not quenched.

---

[36] *geenna* 12x pr. *the valley of Hinnom*, south of Jerusalem, once celebrated for the horrid worship of Moloch, and afterwards polluted with every species of filth, as well as the carcasses of animals, and dead bodies of malefactors; to consume which, in order to avert the pestilence which such a mass of corruption would occasion, constant fires were kept burning. – MCEDONTW

About one year later, Nisan 11th 33 C.E. on the Mount of Olives, Jesus spoke prophetically of a future time when he would say to the wicked,

Matthew 25:41, 46 English Standard Version (ESV)	**Matthew 25:41, 46** New American Standard Bible (NASB)
41 "Then he will say to those on his left, 'Depart from me, you cursed, into the eternal fire prepared for the devil and his angels. 46 And these will go away into eternal punishment, but the righteous into eternal life."	41 "Then He will also say to those on His left, 'Depart from Me, accursed ones, into the eternal fire which has been prepared for the devil and his angels; 46 These will go away into eternal punishment, but the righteous into eternal life."

If we were to take Jesus' words in the above in isolation without looking at the Bible backgrounds or any of the original language words, it might seem like Jesus was teaching a hellfire doctrine of eternal torment. However, this would contradict other parts of Scripture that clearly teaches the punishment of eternal destruction." – 2 Thessalonians 1:9, ESV.

What did Jesus mean in the above text when he said people would be 'thrown into hell?' How are we to understand "the eternal fire" that Jesus warned us about, is it literal or symbolic? The original Greek word translated "hell" at Mark 9:47 is Geenna.

Gehenna Hebrew Ge' Hinnom, literally, valley of Hinnom appears 12 times in the Greek New Testament books, and many translators render it by the word "hell." Most translations have chosen poorly <u>not to</u> use a transliteration, Gehenna or Geenna, as opposed to the English hell, ASV, AT, RSV, ESV, LEB, HCSB, and NASB. There is little doubt that the New Testament writers and Jesus used "Gehenna" to speak of the place of final punishment. What was Gehenna?

According to the Holman Illustrated Bible Dictionary (p. 632), Gehenna or the Valley of Hinnom was "the valley south of Jerusalem now called the *Wadi er-Rababi* (Josh. 15:8; 18:16; 2 Chron. 33:6; Jer. 32:35) became the place of child sacrifice to foreign gods. The Jews later used the valley for the dumping of refuse, the dead bodies of animals, and executed criminals."[37] We would disagree with the other comments by the Holman Illustrated Dictionary, "The continuing fires in the valley (to consume the refuse and dead bodies) apparently led the people to transfer the name to the place where the wicked dead suffer." This just is not the case.

---

[37] Chad Brand, Charles Draper, et al., eds., "Gehenna," *Holman Illustrated Bible Dictionary* (Nashville, TN: Holman Bible Publishers, 2003), 631.

In the Old Testament, the Israelites did burn sons in the fires as part of a sacrifice to false gods, but not for the purpose of punishment or torture. By the time of the New Testament period, hundreds of years later, the only thing thrown in Gehenna was trash and the dead bodies of executed criminals. For what purpose were these thrown into Gehenna? It was used as an incinerator, a furnace for destroying things by burning them. Notice that any bodies thrown in Gehenna during the New Testament period were already dead. Thus, if anything, these people saw Gehenna as a place where they destroyed their trash and the bodies of dead criminals. Thus, if Jesus used this to illustrate as the place of the wicked, it would have represented destruction as the punishment.

The Valley of Slaughter

Jeremiah 7:30-34 English Standard Version (ESV)

[30] "For the sons of Judah have done evil in my sight, declares the Lord. They have set their detestable things in the house that is called by my name, to defile it. [31] And they have built the high places of Topheth, which is in the Valley of the Son of Hinnom, to burn their sons and their daughters in the fire, which I did not command, **nor did it come into my mind**. [32] Therefore, behold, the days are coming, declares the Lord, when it will no more be called Topheth, or the Valley of the Son of Hinnom, but the Valley of Slaughter; for they will

bury in Topheth, because there is no room elsewhere. 33 And the dead bodies of this people will be food for the birds of the air, and for the beasts of the earth, and none will frighten them away. 34 And I will silence in the cities of Judah and in the streets of Jerusalem the voice of mirth and the voice of gladness, the voice of the bridegroom and the voice of the bride, for the land shall become a waste.

This valley of Hinnom was on the outskirts of ancient Jerusalem. As we can see from the above text in Jeremiah, it was used for the practice of child sacrifice, a sickening and abhorrent practice that God condemned. God had said the idea of burning someone alive, 'did even come into his mind,' and he would execute such ones, not even torture these wicked ones. Therefore, God foretold that the Valley of Hinnom would become a place for the destruction of dead bodies, not to torture live victims.

Jesus reference to 'the worms that eat them never die, and the fire that burns them is never put out,' he was alluding to Isaiah 66:24. (See cross-reference NASB) Regarding "the corpses of the men Who have transgressed against [God]," Isaiah says that "their worm will not die And their fire will not be quenched." (NASB) Those listening to Jesus would have been very familiar with the book of Isaiah, knowing his reference was to the treatment of "the corpses of the men," who did not deserve to be buried.

Thus, it is all too clear that Jesus was using the Valley of Hinnom, or Gehenna, as a symbol of eternal destruction for those who would never receive a resurrection. He made this, even more, clear when he said, "fear [God] who is able to destroy both soul and body in hell [Gr Gehenna]." (Matt. 10:28, NASB) Therefore, Gehenna is a symbol of eternal death, not eternal torment in some eternal hellfire.

What about Jesus mention of "the eternal fire," is it literal or symbolic? (Matt 25:41) If we look at the whole verse, we can see that this eternal fire is "prepared for the devil and his angels." Is it possible for literal fire to burn spirit persons? Clearly, Jesus was using symbolism here, as we also consider the fact that the mention of "the sheep" and "the goats" mentioned in the same section of verses are not literal. The sheep and the goats are word pictures used to symbolize two groups of peoples. (Matt. 25:32-33) The "eternal fire" that Jesus spoke of is used as a symbol for the burning up of the wicked in a figurative sense.

Well, some might ask, what about the wicked, who "will go away into eternal punishment"? First, eternal punishment does not automatically equate into eternal torment by eternal fire.

The basic meaning of the Greek word *kolasin* "akin to kolazoo,"[38] "means 'to cut short,'

---

[38] W. E. Vire, Merrill F. Unger, and William White Jr., Vine's Complete Expository Dictionary of Old and

'to lop,' 'to trim,' and figuratively a. 'to impede,' 'restrain,' and b. 'to punish,' and in the passive 'to suffer loss.'[39] The first part of the sentence is only in harmony with the second part of the sentence, if the eternal punishment is eternal death. The wicked receive eternal death and the righteous eternal life. We might at that Matthews Gospel was primarily for the Jewish Christians, and under the Mosaic Law, God would punish those who violated the law, saying they "shall be cut off [penalty of death] from Israel." (Ex 12:15; Lev 20:2-3) We need further to consider,

2 Thessalonians 1:8-9 English Standard Version (ESV)

[8] in flaming fire, inflicting vengeance on those who do not know God and on those who do not obey the gospel of our Lord Jesus. [9] They will suffer **the punishment of eternal destruction**, away from the presence of the Lord and from the glory of his might

Notice that Paul says too that the punishment for the wicked is "eternal destruction." Many times in talking with those that support the position of eternal torment in some hellfire, they will add a

---

New Testament Words (Nashville, TN: T. Nelson, 1996), 498.

[39] Gerhard Kittel, Gerhard Friedrich, and Geoffrey William Bromiley, *Theological Dictionary of the New Testament* (Grand Rapids, MI: W.B. Eerdmans, 1985), 451.

word to Matthew 25:46 in their paraphrase of the verse, 'conscious eternal punishment.' However, Jesus does not tell us what the eternal punishment is, just that it is a punishment and it is eternal. Therefore, those who support eternal conscious fiery torment will read the verse to mean just that, while those, who hold the position of eternal destruction, will take Matthew 25:46 to mean that. Considering that Jesus does not define what the eternal punishment is, this verse is not a proof text for either side of the argument.

Therefore, Jesus did not teach that God was going to torture the wicked in some eternal hellfire forever. Rather, Jesus said, "God so loved the world, that He gave His only begotten Son, that whoever believes in Him shall not perish, but have eternal life." (John 3:16, NASB) Implied in this verse is if we think we will receive eternal life, if we do not, we will not, which means we will die. If Jesus meant that, the wicked received eternal life of another kind, suffering torment in a fiery hell, why not state so here. Rather, he says, if 'we do not believe, we will perish.' Let us look at verse 36, which informs us what the believer and the unbeliever will receive, "He who believes in the Son has eternal life; but he who does not obey the Son will not see life, but the wrath of God abides on him." If we refuse to accept Jesus, then we will not receive life. One has to be alive to receive eternal torment in some hellfire.

Short History of Hell as Eternal Torment

Greek Mythology (900 – 500 B.C.E.)

The *Encarta Encyclopedia* says, "**Hades**, in Greek mythology, god of the dead. He was the son of the Titans Cronus and Rhea and the brother of Zeus and Poseidon. When the three brothers divided up the universe after they had deposed their father, Cronus, Hades was awarded the underworld. There, with his queen, Persephone, whom he had abducted from the world above, he ruled the kingdom of the dead. Although he was a grim and pitiless god, unappeased by either prayer or sacrifice, he was not evil. In fact, he was known also as Pluto, lord of riches, because both crops and precious metals were believed to come from his kingdom below ground."

"The underworld itself was often called Hades. It was divided into two regions: Erebus, where the dead pass as soon as they die, and Tartarus, the deeper region, where the Titans had been imprisoned. It was a dim and unhappy place, inhabited by vague forms and shadows and guarded by Cerberus, the three-headed, dragon-tailed dog. Sinister rivers separated the underworld from the world above, and the aged boatman Charon ferried the souls of the dead across these waters. Somewhere in the darkness of the underworld Hades' palace was located. It was represented as a many-gated, dark and gloomy place, thronged with guests, and set in the midst of shadowy fields and an apparition-haunted landscape. In later legends the underworld is described as the place where the good are rewarded and the wicked punished."

"**Eurydice**, in Greek mythology, a beautiful nymph, and wife of Orpheus, the master musician. Shortly after their marriage Eurydice was bitten in the foot by a snake and died. Grief-stricken, Orpheus descended into the underworld to seek his wife. Accompanying his song with the strains of his lyre, he begged Hades, god of the dead, to relinquish Eurydice. His music so touched Hades that Orpheus was permitted to take his wife back with him on the condition that he would not turn around to look at her until they had reached the upper air. They had almost completed their ascent when Orpheus, overwhelmed by love and anxiety, looked back to see if Eurydice was following him. The promise broken, Eurydice vanished forever to the regions of the dead."

"**Tartarus**, in Greek mythology, the lowest region of the underworld. According to Hesiod and Virgil, Tartarus is as far below Hades as the earth is below the heavens and is closed in by iron gates. In some accounts Zeus, the father of the gods, after leading the gods to victory over the Titans, banished his father, Cronus, and the other Titans to Tartarus. The name Tartarus was later employed sometimes as a synonym for Hades, or the underworld in general, but more frequently for the place of damnation where the wicked were punished after death. Such legendary sinners as

Ixion, king of the Lapiths, Sisyphus, king of Corinth, and Tantalus, a mortal son of Zeus, were placed in Tartarus."

Scandinavian Mythology (450 B.C.E. – 100 C.E.

The *Encarta Encyclopedia* says, "Many ancient mythological heroes, some of whom may have been derived from real persons, were believed to be descendants of the gods; among them were Sigurd the Dragon-slayer; Helgi Thrice-Born, Harald Wartooth, Hadding, Starkad, and the Valkyries. The Valkyries, a band of warrior-maidens that included Svava and Brunhild, served Odin as choosers of slain warriors, who were taken to reside in Valhalla. There the warriors would spend their days fighting and nights feasting until Ragnarok, the day of the final world battle, in which the old gods would perish and a new reign of peace and love would be instituted. Ordinary individuals were received after death by the goddess Hel in a cheerless underground world."

Zoroastrianism Mythology (650 - 330 B.C.E.

The *Encarta Encyclopedia* says, "**Zoroastrianism**, religion that arose from the teachings of the devotional poet Zoroaster, known as Zarathushtra to ancient Iranians, who is regarded as the faith's founding prophet. Scholars believe that Zoroaster lived sometime between 1750 and 1500 BC or 1400 and 1200 BC. The Zoroastrian scripture, called the Avesta, includes poems attributed to Zoroaster. The religion continues to be practiced today by Zoroastrian communities in India, Iran, the United States, Canada, and other countries."

"Zoroastrians believe that Ahura Mazda created humans as allies in the cosmic struggle against evil and that humanity will be resurrected and granted immortality once evil has been defeated. They further view the material world as a trap into which evil has been lured and in which evil will undergo defeat by divinities and humans working together. Zoroastrianism preaches that when someone dies his or her soul undergoes individual judgment based on actions while alive. If the soul's good deeds are greater than its evil deeds, it enters paradise. If the soul's evil deeds outweigh the good done while alive, it is cast into hell to await the day of universal judgment. In cases where a soul's good deeds equal its evil deeds, it is consigned to limbo."

"Close to the end of time a savior will resurrect the dead, Zoroastrianism claims. Ahura Mazda will descend to earth with the other good spirits. Each sinner, having already suffered in hell or limbo after death, will be purified. Thereafter, immortality will be granted to all humans. Ahura Mazda, the holy immortals, and other divine beings will annihilate the demons and force Angra Mainyu to scuttle back into hell, which will then be sealed."

"The Zoroastrian doctrine of heaven, hell, and limbo influenced other faiths. Islam absorbed not only the ideas of heaven, hell, and limbo, but also the scheme of individual judgment at a celestial bridge and the notion of final, universal judgment. Christianity further assimilated the Zoroastrian belief of the soul's afterlife and the appearance of a savior, resurrection, and eternal life at the end of the world. "[40]

Learning the Truth About Hell

Church leaders who teach that hell is is a place of some fiery torment where the wicked burn for eternity are supporting a gross distortion of God and his qualities. True enough, the Bible does say that God will destroy the wicked. (2 Thess. 1:6-9) Nevertheless, God's righteous indignation is not such, that it becomes unjust, out of balance with his other qualities.

God is not hateful, spiteful or bitter. He asks, "Do I have any pleasure in the death of the wicked?" (Eze. 18:23, NASB) Think it through, if God has no please in the death of the wick, how are we to believe he would find justice, joy, happiness, and delight in an eternity of horrific torture? God's outstanding quality is love. (1 John 4:8) He has even commanded us to love our enemies (Matt 5:44), i.e., be willing to share the gospel with them if their heart condition should change. This mindset seems completely out of place with the idea of eternal torment.

---

[40] Microsoft ® Encarta ® 2006. © 1993-2005 Microsoft Corporation. All rights reserved.

Being Released from Hell?

Much confusion and misunderstanding has been caused through some Bible translations like the King James Version, which renders all of our original language words as hell: *Sheol*, *Hades*, *Gehenna*, and *Tartarus*. If we have a correct understanding of Gehenna and Hades, we will discover a truth that we never knew before. *Gehenna* is pictorial of a place where the dead go, who receive total destruction, with no hope of a resurrection, as *Gehenna* was an incinerator. *Hades*, on the other hand, is the grave, where there is the hope of a future resurrection.

After Jesus died and was resurrected, the apostle Peter stated the following about Jesus,

Acts 2:27 English Standard Version (ESV)

²⁷ For you will not abandon my soul to Hades **[hell KJV]**,
  or let your Holy One see corruption.

Acts 2:31-32 English Standard Version (ESV)

³¹ he foresaw and spoke about the resurrection of the Christ, that he was not abandoned to Hades **[hell KJV]**, nor did his flesh see corruption. ³² This Jesus God raised up, and of that we all are witnesses.

Peter was quoting Psalm 16:10 in verse 31 of Acts 2, where he clearly stated Jesus was resurrected from hades,

Psalm 16:10 English Standard Version (ESV)

¹⁰ For you will not abandon my soul to Sheol **[hell KJV]**,
   or let your holy one see corruption.

As we can see the transliteration of original language word, in Psalm is *Sheol* and in Acts, it is *Hades*, which is rendered by just one word in the King James Version. The King James Version renders *Sheol* as "hell," "the grave," and "the pit;" *Hades* is therein rendered both "hell" and "grave;" *Gehenna* is also translated "hell;" and *Tartarus* is rendered as "hell." When Jesus was in Hades for three days, he was not in some fiery place of torment. *Hades* [hell KJV] was the grave from which Jesus received a resurrection. Moreover, Jesus is not the only person who will receive a resurrection from Hades [hell KJV].

In connection with the resurrection, the Bible says, "Death and Hades **[hell KJV]** gave up the dead who were in them." (Rev. 20:13, 14, ESV) Here we see God emptying Hades, i.e., hell, which will mean that those who are worthy will be restored to life in a resurrection. (John 5:28-29; Acts 24:15) This is the great hope that should be in every Christian heart and mind, seeing those that we loved return from Hades [hell, KJV], namely, the grave! The God of infinite love will carry this out.

CHAPTER 5 The Wicked Will Be No More

Psalm 37:10 Updated Standard Version (ESV)

¹⁰ Just a little while longer and the wicked one will be no more;

And you will look carefully for his place and he will not be there.

As we have seen through this publication, the punishment for those who reject Jesus Christ is total destruction rather than everlasting torment. This directly related to the soul [Heb. *nephesh*, Gr *psyche*] is the person ("man became a living soul," Gen 2:7, ASV), who has lost everlasting life, and the only way to have everlasting life restored is by way of our accepting the sovereignty of God. The doctrinal position of annihilationism is the complete destruction of the soul, i.e., the wicked person, which leaves the righteous with everlasting life.

Interpretation of Scripture

Those investigating the Scriptures must ask themselves, 'why would God use words like "destroy, destruction, perish, death" to mean something other than their plain meaning? This seems to fly in the face of the idea that the soul goes to some place of eternal torment, but rather are terminated by their destruction.

Psalm 1:6	... the way of the wicked will *perish*
Psalm 37:20	But the wicked will *perish*... the enemies of the Lord will be like the glory of the pastures, They vanish—like smoke they vanish away.
Psalm 92:7	evildoers flourish, ... are doomed to *destruction forever*
Matthew 10:28b	Rather fear him who can *destroy* both soul and body in hell.
John 3:16	... whoever believes in him should not perish (Gr destroyed) but have eternal life. ...
John 3:36	whoever does not obey the Son *shall not see life*, but the wrath of God remains on him.
Rom. 6:23	For the wages of sin is *death* ...
Phil. 3:19	whose end is "destruction" ...
2 Thess. 1:9	These will pay the penalty of eternal *destruction* ...

Hebrews 10:39	But we are not of those who shrink back and are *destroyed*, but of those who have faith and preserve their souls.
James 4:12a	There is only one lawgiver and judge, he who is able to save and to *destroy*.
Rev. 20:14	This is the second death...

There is little doubt that the most difficult thing any human has to suffer through is death. However, for the wicked, who have rejected the sovereignty of God that is the extent of their pain and suffering, knowing that live is no more. The wages of sin is death, not eternal existence.

Hebrews 10:26-27 English Standard Version (ESV)

26 For if we go on sinning deliberately after receiving the knowledge of the truth, there no longer remains a sacrifice for sins, 27 but a fearful expectation of judgment, and a fury of fire that will **consume the adversaries**.

The apostle Paul speaks of a figurative "fury of fire that will *consume* the adversaries." The *Greek-English Lexicon of the New Testament* says, "(a figurative extension of meaning of ἐσθίω 'to eat,'

23.1) to destroy, with the implication of doing away with all traces of an object—'to destroy, to consume.'"[41]

2 Peter 3:7 English Standard Version (ESV)

[7] But by the same word the heavens and earth that now exist are stored up for fire, being kept until the day of judgment and **destruction of the ungodly**.

Peter tells us that the *ungodly will be destroyed*. The *Greek-English Lexicon of the New Testament* says, "to destroy or to cause the destruction of persons, objects, or institutions—'to ruin, to destroy, destruction.'"[42]

Some may wonder, though, about 2 Peter 3:7a. It says, "The heavens and earth that now exist are stored up for fire." Does this not support that the earth "shall be burned up"[43] (2 Pet. 3:10) as the KJV says. Does this not show that the earth will be burned up? See the footnote below, the reading *heurethesetai*, "be disclosed, "be exposed," or "be discovered" is the preferred reading. *Katakaesetai*

---

[41] Johannes P. Louw and Eugene Albert Nida, *Greek-English Lexicon of the New Testament: Based on Semantic Domains* (New York: United Bible Societies, 1996), 232.

[42] IBID, 231.

[43] The preferred is "be exposed" or "be disclosed," (א B K P 424ᶜ 1175 1739ᵗˣᵗ 1852 syrᵖʰ·ʰᵐᵍ arm Origen; while the less preferred reading is "be burned up," A 048 049 056 0142 33 614 *Byz Lect* syrʰ copᵇᵒ eth *al*

(KJV), "be burned up" is the inferior reading and is not preferred. Moreover, the Bible sometimes uses the terms "heavens," "earth," and "fire" figuratively, as symbols. For example, at Genesis 11:1, it reads, "Now the whole earth had one language and the same words." Here we see Moses uses the word "earth" in a figurative sense, to mean all of human society.

Romans 2:7 English Standard Version (ESV)

⁷ to those who by patience in well-doing seek for glory and honor and immortality, he will give eternal life;

Paul tells us here that it is only the righteous, who will receive eternal life. Certainly, to suffer eternal torment is eternal life, which would contradict this verse.

Genesis 3:19 English Standard Version (ESV)

¹⁹ By the sweat of your face
    you shall eat bread,
till you return to the ground,
    for out of it you were taken;
for you are dust,
    and to dust you shall return."

God had made Adam from the dust of the ground. (Gen. 2:7) Adam had not been in existence prior to God creating him. Therefore, when God said that Adam would return to the dust, he meant that Adam was going to return to that nonexistent state. In other words, Adam would be as lifeless as the dust from which he had come.

Psalm 146:4 Young's Literal Translation (YLT)

⁴ His spirit goes forth; he returns to his earth, In that day have his thoughts perished.

Are we to understand that there is some spiritual being within us, which then departs from us at death? No, this is not the understanding, as the Psalmist next words were, "In that day have his thoughts perished," ("all his thinking ends," *NEB*). How, then, are we to understand this verse?

In the Hebrew Scriptures, we have *ruach*, and in the Greek New Testament, we have *pneuma*, both with the basic meaning "breath." This is why other translations read, "His breath goes forth."

Psalm 146:4	Psalm 146:4	Psalm 146:4
(ESV)	(LEB)	(HCSB)
⁴ When his **breath departs**, he returns to the earth; on that very day his plans perish.	⁴ His **breath departs**; he returns to his plot; on that day his plans perish.	⁴ When his **breath leaves** him, he returns to the ground; on that day his plans die.

We will notice this further clarified when Moses informs us of what took place at the flood. However, we look at the literal translations first, followed by other literal translations that choose to define the use of the term "spirit." Note how we will use a footnote in the literal, and the others that chose to define.

Genesis 7:22 (NASB)	Genesis 7:22 (ASV)	Genesis 7:22 (YLT)
22 of all that was on the dry land, all in whose nostrils was the breath of the spirit of life **[breath of life]**, died.	22 all in whose nostrils was the breath of the spirit of life **[breath of life]**, of all that was on the dry land, died.	22 all in whose nostrils [is] breath of a living spirit **[breath of life]** -- of all that [is] in the dry land -- have died.

Other literal and semi-literal translations,

Genesis 7:22 (ESV)	Genesis 7:22 (LEB)	Genesis 7:22 (NRSV)
22 Everything on the dry land in whose nostrils was the breath of life **["a breath of spirit of life"]** died.	22 Everything in whose nostrils *was the breath of life* **["a breath of spirit of life"]**, among all that *was* on dry land, died.	22 everything on dry land in whose nostrils was the breath of life **["a breath of spirit of life"]** died.

Therefore, "*ruach*" and "pneuma," i.e., "spirit" can refer to the breath of life that is active within both human and animal creatures. Then how do we explain Ecclesiastes 12:7?

Ecclesiastes 12:7 English Standard Version (ESV)

⁷ and the dust returns to the earth as it was, and the spirit returns to God who gave it.

Are we to understand that a spiritual being within us, leaves us at death, and returns to God? No. We just learned that the "spirit" is the "breath of life," which sustains human and animal life. Once we lose our "breath of life," and are dead, the only hope of having it restored comes from God. Therefore, "the spirit returns to God," in that our only hope for living again, but this time for eternally, comes from God. It is only God, who can restore the "breath of life," which allows us to live again. Keep in mind too, this person was never in heaven with God, so the idea of him as a spirit person returning to God is not what is meant. How can he return to God, if he was never in heaven with God to begin with? Again, it is the "breath of life," which enables the person to live that returns to God, not literally, but in the sense of his having the power to restore it.

Ecclesiastes 12:7 (LEB)	**Ecclesiastes 12:7** (NRSV)
⁷ And the dust returns to the earth as it	⁷ and the dust returns to the earth as it was, and the

was, and the breath returns to God who gave it.	breath returns to God who gave it.

All conservative Christians would point to the Bible as the final authority on all doctrine. This is true of our understanding of the *soul* as well. In the Hebrew Old Testament, the Hebrew word *nephesh* (translated "soul" in the UASV) is found 754 times, first in Genesis 1:20. In the Greek New Testament, the Greek word *psuche* (translated "soul" in the UASV) is found by itself 102 times, first in Matthew 2:20. In each case, a literal translation, looking to give its readers what God had said, should render this Hebrew and Greek word "soul," with the interpretive rendering in the footnote. By doing this, the reader of the Bible will be able to see how the word "soul" is used within the whole of the inspired, inerrant Word of God.

What is the Condition of the Dead?

When the Bible talks about the condition of the dead it presents it in five senses, (1) knowing nothing, (2) asleep like state, (3) powerless, (4) returning to the dust of the ground, (5) and awaiting a resurrection. If we examine both the Bible and religious history, the belief that a soul or spirit within us lives on after our physical death originates with Socrates and Plato. However, was it not Satan, who argued clear back in the Garden of Eden to Eve, saying that "You will not surely die."?

(Gen. 3:4, ESV) Yes, it was Satan that implied that Eve would not die in the flesh if she ignored God's prohibition on the tree og knowledge of good and bad.

First Sense

Ecclesiastes 9:5, 10 English Standard Version (ESV)

⁵ For the living know that they will die, but the dead know nothing, and they have no more reward, for the memory of them is forgotten. ¹⁰ Whatever your hand finds to do, do it with your might, for there is no work or thought or knowledge or wisdom in Sheol [gravedom], to which you are going.

Second Sense

John 11:11 (ESV)	1 Kings 2:10 (ESV)
¹¹ After saying these things, he said to them, "Our friend Lazarus has fallen asleep, but I go to awaken him."	¹⁰ Then David slept with his fathers and was buried in the city of David.

Third Sense

Proverbs 2:18 (ESV)	Isaiah 26:14 (ESV)

¹⁸ for her house sinks down to death,
    and her paths to the departed;
	¹⁴ They are dead, they will not live;
	    they are shades, they will not arise;
	to that end you have

	visited them with destruction and wiped out all remembrance of them.

Fourth Sense

Genesis 3:19 (ESV)	Ecclesiastes 3:19-20 (NASB)

19 By the sweat of your face
    you shall eat bread,
till you return to the ground,
    for out of it you were taken;
for you are dust,
    and to dust you shall return."
	19 For the fate of the sons of men and the fate of beasts is the same. As one dies so dies the other; indeed, they all have the same breath and there is no advantage for man over beast, for all is vanity. 20 All go to the same place. All came from the dust and all return to the dust.

Fifth Sense

John 5:28-29 (ESV)	Acts 24:15 (ESV)
28 Do not marvel at this, for an hour is coming when all who are in the tombs will hear his voice 29 and come out, those who have done good to the resurrection of life, and those who have done evil to the resurrection of judgment.	15 having a hope in God, which these men themselves accept, that there will be a resurrection of both the just and the unjust.

In death, Scripture shows us as being unable to praise God. The Psalmist tells us, "For in death there is no remembrance of you; in Sheol [gravedom] who will give you praise?" (Psa. 6:5) Isaiah the prophet writes, "For Sheol [gravedom] cannot thank you [God], death cannot praise you; those who go down to the pit cannot hope for your faithfulness. 'It is the living who give thanks to you, as I do today; a father tells his sons about your faithfulness.'" – Isaiah 38:18-19.

Can the Soul Die?

When we die, what happens to the soul? If you recall from above that the "soul" is the person, the being, the creature, i.e., us, and the **life** that we have. If you recall from above, the **Human soul =** body **[dust of the ground] +** active life force **("spirit") [Hebrew, *ruach*]** within the trillions of human cells which make up the human body + breath of life [Hebrew, *neshamah*] that sustains the life force from God. In other words, the "soul" is we as a whole, everything that we are, so the soul or we humans can die. Let us look at a few verses, which make that all too clear.

Ecclesiastes 3:19-20 New American Standard Bible (NASB)

¹⁹ For the fate of the sons of men **[humans or people]** and the fate of beasts is the same. As one dies so dies the other; indeed, they all have the same breath and there is no advantage for man over beast, for all is vanity. ²⁰ All go to the same

place. All came from the dust and all return to the dust.

In other words, when we breathe our last breath, our cells begin to die. Death is the ending of all vital functions or processes in an organism or cell. When our heart stops beating, our blood is no longer circulating, carrying nourishment and oxygen (by breathing) to the trillions of cells in our body; we are what are termed, clinically dead. However, somatic death has yet to occur, meaning we can be revived, after many minutes of being clinically dead, if the heart and lungs can be restarted again, which gives the cells the oxygen they need.

After about three minutes of clinical death, the brain cells begin to die, meaning the chances of reviving the person is less likely as each second passes. We know that it is vital that the breathing and blood flow be maintained for the life force (*ruach chaiyim*) in the cells. Nevertheless, it is not the lack of breathing or the failure of the heart beating alone, but rather the active life force **("spirit") [Hebrew, ruach]** within the trillions of human cells which make up the human body + breath of life [Hebrew, *neshamah*] that sustains the life force from God.

Ps.104:29 (ESV)	Ps. 146:4 (ESV)	Eccl. 8:8 (ESV)
²⁹ When you hide your face, they are dismayed; when you take away their	⁴ When his breath departs, he returns to the earth; on that very	⁸ No man has power to retain the spirit, or power over the day of death.

breath, they die and return to their dust.	day his plans perish.	There is no discharge from war, nor will wickedness deliver those who are given to it.

Again, ...

Ezekiel 18:4	**Leviticus 21:1**	**Numbers 6:6**
(ESV)	(ASV)	(ASV)
4 Behold, all souls are mine; the soul of the father as well as the soul of the son is mine: the soul who sins shall die.	21 And Jehovah said to Moses, Speak to the priests, the sons of Aaron, and say to them, There shall none defile himself for the dead **[Or "for a soul."]** among his people;	6 All the days that he separates himself unto Jehovah he shall not come near to a dead body **[Or "soul."]**.

Again, the death of a "soul" means the death of a person ...

1 Kings 19:4	Jonah 4:8	Mark 3:4
(ASV)	(ASV)	(ASV)
4 But he himself went a day's journey into the wilderness, and came and sat down under a juniper-tree: and he requested for himself that he **[Or "his soul.]** "might die, and said, It is enough; now, O Jehovah, take away my life [soul]; for I am not better than my fathers.	8 And it came to pass, when the sun arose, that God prepared a sultry east wind; and the sun beat upon the head of Jonah, that he fainted, and requested for himself that he might die **[Or "that his soul might die."]**, and said, It is better for me to die than to live.	4 And he said to them, Is it lawful on the sabbath day to do good, or to do harm? to save a life **[Or "soul."]**, or to kill? But they held their peace.

As you can see from the above texts, a "soul," or person can die. However, how are we to understand those texts that say the "soul" went out of a person, or came back into a person?

Soul Departing and Soul Coming into a Person

Genesis 35:18 English Standard Version (ESV)

18 And as her soul was departing (for she was dying), she called his name Ben-oni; but his father called him Benjamin.

Are we to understand from this that Rachel had some inner being, a soul, which departed from her at death? No. We will recall from the texts from above that the term "soul" can also be used in reference to the life one has. Thus, this is a reference to her life that she had leaving her. Note the *Lexham English Bible*, "And it happened *that* when **her life was departing** (for she was dying), she called his name Ben-Oni. But his father called him Benjamin." (Bold and underline is mine) Therefore, it was her "life" that she had, which departed from her, not some inner being. When we take the time to ponder these things, it becomes all the more clear.

1 Kings 17:22 American Standard Version (ASV)

²² And Jehovah listened to the voice of Elijah; and the soul of the child came into him again, and he revived.

Here again, the word "soul" is the "life" that someone has. The *New American Standard Bible* reads, "The **life** of the child returned to him and he revived." The *Lexham English Bible* reads, "The **life** of the child returned within him, and he lived." The *Holman Christian Standard Bible* reads, "The boy's **life** returned to him, and he lived." (Bold is mine)

John 11:11 (ESV)	**1 Kings 2:10** (ESV)
¹¹ After saying these things, he said to them, "Our friend Lazarus has fallen asleep, but I go to awaken him."	¹⁰ Then David slept with his fathers and was buried in the city of David.

Notice that Lazarus' death is equated with being asleep in death, while King David is referred to as sleeping in death. This gives the reader a hope, as just as easily as you and I can awaken a person from sleep, Jesus is going to awaken people from death, a death like sleep. We are going to look at these verses a little differently that we have with the others. We will pause for a moment to see how a literal translation is best (which has already been demonstrated), with an interpretation in a footnote. Moreover, it is important that we read those footnotes. Otherwise, we can come to the wrong conclusions.

CHAPTER 6 The Hope of a Resurrection - Where?

All of us have lost a loved one to this force to be reckoned with, and it is only a matter of time before we have to face the greatest enemy humankind has ever known, death! However, we have been given a hope that is as great at the penalty that we are under. We have the hope of life eternal, and if we die, it is the hope of a resurrection. This hope means that we will be reunited with the loved ones that we have lost. Some in the past have had a foretaste of this great hope:

Mark 5:35, 41-42 English Standard Version (ESV)

35 While he was still speaking, there came from the ruler's house some who said, "Your daughter is dead. Why trouble the Teacher any further?" **41** Taking her by the hand he said to her, "Talitha cumi," which means, "Little girl, I say to you, arise." **42** And immediately the girl got up and began walking (for she was twelve years of age), and they were immediately overcome with amazement.

Acts 9:36-41 English Standard Version (ESV)

36 Now there was in Joppa a disciple named Tabitha, which, translated, means Dorcas.[44] She was

---

[44] The Aramaic name Tabitha and the Greek name Dorcas both mean gazelle

full of good works and acts of charity. **37** In those days she became ill and died, and when they had washed her, they laid her in an upper room. **38** Since Lydda was near Joppa, the disciples, hearing that Peter was there, sent two men to him, urging him, "Please come to us without delay." **39** So Peter rose and went with them. And when he arrived, they took him to the upper room. All the widows stood beside him weeping and showing tunics[45] and other garments that Dorcas made while she was with them. **40** But Peter put them all outside, and knelt down and prayed; and turning to the body he said, "Tabitha, arise." And she opened her eyes, and when she saw Peter she sat up. **41** And he gave her his hand and raised her up. Then calling the saints and widows, he presented her alive.

We have already heard of the charges that Satan has risen against God in chapter six of this book. The resurrection hope allows God to let Satan play out his challenges, to resolve the issues that would have otherwise plagued us for an eternity. It is like when you suffer through a painful medical treatment, to enjoy thereafter with all the complications of the issues you had. It is only by means of the greatest resurrection, namely Jesus Christ that we can have this hope.

---

[45] Greek chiton, a long garment worn under the cloak next to the skin

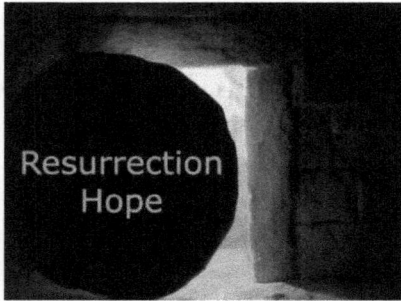

Resurrection Hope

Matthew 20:28
English Standard Version (ESV)

²⁸ even as the Son of Man came not to be served but to serve, and to give his life as a ransom for many.

Resurrection is a Foundational Doctrine

Hebrews 6:1-2 English Standard Version (ESV)

⁶ Therefore let us leave the elementary doctrine of Christ and go on to maturity, not laying again a foundation of repentance from dead works and of faith toward God, ² and of instruction about washings,⁴⁶ the laying on of hands, the resurrection of the dead and eternal judgment.

The resurrection is a foundational doctrine of our Christian faith. However, it does not fit into the world of humankind that is alienated from God. They see this as the only life there is, and so they are in pursuit of fleshly pleasures, to make the most of it. The mindset of some of the first century was, "If the dead are not raised, 'Let us eat and drink, for tomorrow we die.'" (1 Cor. 15:32, ESV) We, on the other hand, do not need to chase after the things that Satan's world has to offer.

---

⁴⁶ Or baptisms (that is, cleansing rites)

Acts 17:32 English Standard Version (ESV)

³² Now when they heard of the resurrection of the dead, some mocked. But others said, "We will hear you again about this."

We need to look to at least two **hopes** that humans have the opportunity of having. Some are of new Israel and is seen as being given a kingdom, a chosen race, a royal priesthood, and ruling with Christ for a thousand years. There will be a need to investigate this, and this section will be a little more complex than any other part of this book. It is very important to all of us, so bear with me. I am going to quote some of the leading evangelical scholars at length.

Revelation 5:9-10 English Standard Version (ESV)

⁹ And they **sang <u>a new song</u>**, saying,

"Worthy are you to take the scroll
  and to open its seals,
for you were slain, and by your blood you
ransomed people for God
  from every tribe and language and people and
nation,
¹⁰ and **you have made them a kingdom and
priests** to our God,
  and **they shall reign on**⁴⁷ the earth."

---

⁴⁷ According to this verses Jesus will rule "on" the earth. For another consideration, see the next subheading: Over the earth or On the Earth?

A further result of the Lamb's sacrifice is the establishment[48] of the redeemed as a kingdom and priests: *kai epoiēsas autous tǭ theǭ hēmōn basileian kai hiereis* ("and You made them a kingdom and priests to our God"). The threefold occurrence of this theme in Revelation (cf. also Rev. 1:6; 20:6) indicates that talk about such a spiritual heritage was common parlance among Christians of John's day (Swete). As God's possession,[49] the redeemed will not merely be God's people over whom He reigns, but will also share God's rule in the coming millennial kingdom (cf. 1 Cor. 4:8; 6:3) (Charles; Ladd). This kingdom is the goal toward which the program of God is moving as emphasized by *basileusousin* ("they shall reign") later in v. 10 (cf. Rev. 20:4). The idea of priesthood found in *hiereis* ("priests") means full and immediate access into God's presence for the purpose of praise and worship (Ladd). It also includes the thought of priestly service to

---

[48] The aorist ἐποίησας connotes finished result. As commonly the case in the heavenly songs of this book, it is proleptic, anticipating the culmination of the process being carried out at the time the song is sung (Swete, *Apocalypse*, p. 81; Beckwith, *Apocalypse*, pp. 512–13).[48]

[49] Τῷ θεῷ (5:10) has a possessive sense: "belonging to God" as His peculiar people (Beckwith, *Apocalypse*, p. 513).[49]

God (Mounce). Though believers are currently viewed as a royal priesthood (1 Pet. 2:5, 9; cf. Ex. 19:6), this is only preliminary to the fullness of the way they will function alongside Christ in the millennial kingdom.[50]

Kai basileusousin epi tēs gēs ("and they shall reign on the earth") explains more fully the earlier *basileian* ("kingdom"). The fact that believers will serve as reigning powers means that they will be the equivalent of kings (Charles; Beckwith). Spelled out more particularly in 20:4 regarding the millennial kingdom and in 22:5 regarding the eternal state, they will join with Christ in His continual reign following His second advent to the earth. This all stems from the epoch determining redemptive work of the Lamb.[51]

On the earth or Over the Earth

ἐπί epí [2093] is in the genitive and can range from: on, upon; over; at, by; before, in the presence of; when, under, at the time of;[52] Below

---

[50] Newell, Revelation, p. 13.

[51] Robert L. Thomas, Revelation 1-7: An Exegetical Commentary (Chicago: Moody Publishers, 1992), 402.

[52] William D. Mounce, Mounce's Complete Expository Dictionary of Old & New Testament Words (Grand Rapids, MI: Zondervan, 2006), 1150.

you are going to find a list the genitive epi within Revelation that has a similar construction. Please pay special attention to **5:10, 9:11,** and **11:6,** but there will be others that are similar.

If we are to establish that some translations are choosing a rendering because it suits their doctrine, we must compare how they render the same thing elsewhere. You do not need to be a Greek scholar below, so you can ignore the grammar talk, and just notice the similarities and differences.

I do believe that the English is a problem in trying to say, "they shall reign on the earth." First, because this is not a location issue: i.e., where. The genitive *epi* is dealing not with where, but with authority over, which is expressed by having it over _____ not on _____

Please also take special note that the context of all of these epi genitives that follow the active indicative verb and then are followed by the genitive definite article and noun are dealing with authority.

The verb "to reign" is properly used of kings and queens, and here implies complete power over the world and its inhabitants. So another way of expressing this is "and they shall rule over the world and its inhabitants" or "they shall have power over ...."[53]

Rev 5:10: basileusousin epi tēs gēs ("They are reigning [opon, on, over] the earth")[54]

ESV: they shall reign **on** the earth

NASB: they will reign **upon** the earth

ASV: they reign **upon** earth

DBY: they shall reign **over** the earth

ἐπί epí is in the genitive and comes after the future active indicative verb followed by the definite article and followed by a definite genitive article and noun

Rev 9:11: echousin ep autōn basilea (They are having [upon, on, over] them king)

ESV: They have as king **over** them

NASB: They have as king **over** them

ASV: They have **over** them as king

DBT: They have a king **over** them

---

[53] Bratcher, Robert G.; Hatton, Howard: A Handbook on the Revelation to John. New York: United Bible Societies, 1993 (UBS Handbook Series; Helps for Translators), S. 105

[54] English Standard Version (ESV), New American Standard Bible (NASB), American Standard Version (ASV), and the Darby Bible (DBY)

ἐπί epí is in the genitive and comes after the present active indicative verb followed by a definite genitive article and noun

Rev 11:6: exousian echousin epi tōn hudatōn (they are having authority [upon, on, over] the water)

ESV: they have power **over** the waters

NASB: they have power **over** the waters

ASV: they have power **over** the waters

DBY: they have power **over** the waters

ἐπί epí is in the genitive and comes after the future active indicative verb followed by a definite genitive article and noun

Rev 2:26: dōsō autō exousian epi tōn ethnōn (I shall give to him authority [upon, on, over] the nations)

ESV: I will give authority **over** the nations

NASB: I WILL GIVE AUTHORITY **OVER** THE NATIONS

ASV: I give authority **over** the nations

DBY: will I give authority **over** the nations,

ἐπί epí is in the genitive and comes after the future active indicative verb followed by a definite genitive article and noun

Rev 6:8: edothē autois exousia epi to tetarton tēs gēs (was given to them authority [upon, on, over] the fourth of the earth)

ESV: they were given authority **over** a fourth of the earth

NASB: Authority was given to them **over** a fourth of the earth

ASV: here was given unto them authority **over** the fourth part of the earth

DBY: authority was given to him **over** the fourth of the earth

ἐπί **epí** is in the genitive and comes after the future active indicative verb followed by a definite genitive article and noun

Rev 13:7: edothē autō exousia epi pasan phulēn kai laon kai glōssan kai ethnos (was given to it authority [upon, on, over] every tribe and people and tongue and nation)

ESV: authority was given it **over** every tribe and people and language and nation

NASB: authority **over** every tribe and people and tongue and nation was given to him

ASV: there was given to him authority **over** every tribe and people and tongue and nation

DBY: was given to it authority **over** every tribe, and people, and tongue, and nation

ἐπί **epí** is in the genitive and comes after the future active indicative verb followed by a genitive noun. While there is no definite article, it still seems definite in that we know which one: everyone.

Rev 14:18: ho echōn exousian epi tou puros the one having authority [upon, on, over] the fire

ESV: who has authority **over** the fire

NASB: the one who has power **over** fire

ASV: he that hath power **over** fire

DBY: having power **over** fire

Rev 16:9: tou echontos tēn exousian epi pas plēgas (the one having the authority (upon, on, over) the plagues)

ESV: who had power **over** these plagues

NASB: who has the power **over** these plagues

ASV: who hath the power **over** these plagues

DBY: who had authority **over** these plagues

Rev 17:18: hē polis megalē hē echousa basileian epi tōn basileōn tēs gēs (the woman whom you saw is the city the great the one having kingdom (upon, on, over) the kingdoms of the earth)

ESV: the great city that has dominion **over** the kings of the earth

NASB: the great city, which reigns **over** the kings of the earth.

ASV: the great city, which reigneth **over** the kings of the earth.

DBY: the great city, which has kingship **over** the kings of the earth

Revelation 5:9-10 has a high level of theological content. It either says that Jesus and his co-rulers are going to rule from heaven, over the earth or on the earth. It is theological bias to have several cases of similar context and the same grammatical construction, rendering the verses the same every time, yet to then render one verse contrary to the others, simply because it aligns with one's theology. Whether that is the case here or not, the readers will have to determine for themselves. The point regardless is this, either way, Jesus is ruling the earth, and we are blessed to have had his ransom sacrifice and resurrection. Slow down for the next few pages, as things are going to get a little deeper. We can grasp it if we just slow down meditate on what is being said, and get out our dictionary if we have to, and write the definitions in the book beside the word, and read again.

Heavenly Hope

Revelation 14:1-4 English Standard Version (ESV)

¹ Then I looked, and behold, on Mount Zion stood the Lamb, and with him **144,000** who had his name and his Father's name written on

their foreheads. ² And I heard a voice from heaven like the roar of many waters and like the sound of loud thunder. The voice I heard was like the sound of harpists playing on their harps, ³ and **they were singing a <u>new song</u>** before the throne and before the four living creatures and before the elders. <u>**No one could learn that song except the 144,000 who had been redeemed from the earth**</u>. ⁴ It is these who have not defiled themselves with women, for they are virgins. It is these who follow the Lamb wherever he goes. These have been redeemed from mankind as firstfruits for God and the Lamb

The whole of chapter 14 is proleptic. As a summary of the Millennium (20:4–6), the first five verses feature the Lamb in place of the beast, the Lamb's followers with His and the Father's seal in place of the beast's followers with the mark of the beast, and the divinely controlled Mount Zion in place of the pagan-controlled earth (Alford, Moffatt, Kiddle).[55]

Revelation 7:4 English Standard Version (ESV)

⁴ And I heard the number of the sealed, 144,000, sealed from every tribe of the sons of Israel

---

[55] Robert L. Thomas, Revelation 8-22: An Exegetical Commentary (Chicago: Moody Publishers, 1995), 189.

Various efforts have sought to determine the significance of the number 144,000. An understanding of the number as symbolical divides it into three of its multiplicands, 12 × 12 × 1000. From the symbolism of the three it is concluded that the number indicates fixedness and fullest completeness.[56] Twelve, a number of the tribes, is both squared and multiplied by a thousand. This is a twofold way of emphasizing completeness (Mounce). It thus affirms the full number of God's people to be brought through tribulation (Ladd). The symbolic approach points out the impossibility of taking the number literally. It is simply a vast number, less than a number indefinitely great (cf. 7:9), but greater than a large number designedly finite (e.g., 1,000, Rev. 20:2) (Lee). Other occurrences of the numerical components that are supposedly symbolic are also pointed out, 12 thousand in Rev. 21:16, 12 in Rev. 22:2, and 24, a multiple of 12, in Rev. 4:4. This is done to enhance the case for symbolism (Johnson). Though admittedly ingenious, the case for symbolism is exegetically weak. The principal reason for the view is a predisposition to make the 144,000 into a

---

56 Alford, Greek Testament, 4:624; Charles, Revelation, 1:206; Lenski, Revelation, p. 154.

group representative of the church with which no possible numerical connection exists. No justification can be found for understanding the simple statement of fact in v. 4 as a figure of speech. It is a definite number in contrast with the indefinite number of 7:9. If it is taken symbolically, no number in the book can be taken literally. As God reserved 7,000 in the days of Ahab (1 Kings 19:18; Rom. 11:4), He will reserve 144,000 for Himself during the future Great Tribulation.[57] (Thomas, Revelation 1-7: An Exegetical Commentary 1992, 473-74)

These ones are made up of those under the new covenant, the Law of Christ, those **called out of natural Israel**, the new Israelites, also known as the Israel of God. They are a chosen number that

---

[57] Bullinger, Apocalypse, p. 282. Geyser is correct in observing that the predominant concern of the Apocalypse is "the restoration [on earth] of the twelve tribes of Israel, their restoration as a twelve-tribe kingdom, in a renewed and purified city of David, under the rule of the victorious 'Lion of the Tribe of Judah, the Root of David' (5:5; 22:16)" (Albert Geyser, "The Twelve Tribes in Revelation: Judean and Judeo Christian Apocalypticism," NTS 23, no. 3 [July 1982]: 389). He is wrong, however, in his theory that this belief characterized the Judean church only and was not shared by Gentile Christianity spearheaded by Paul (ibid., p. 390).

are to reign with Jesus as kings, priests, and judges. Therefore, we ask, what is the other hope?

The New Earth: The Earthly Hope

In the O[ld] T[estament] the kingdom of God is usually described in terms of a redeemed earth; this is especially clear in the book of Isaiah, where the final state of the universe is already called new heavens and a new earth (65:17; 66:22) The nature of this renewal was perceived only very dimly by OT authors, but they did express the belief that a humans ultimate destiny is an earthly one.[58] This vision is clarified in the N[ew] T[estament]. Jesus speaks of the "renewal" of the world (Matt 19:28), Peter of the restoration of all things (Acts 3:21). Paul writes that the universe will be redeemed by God from its current state of bondage (Rom. 8:18-21). This is confirmed by Peter, who describes the new heavens and the new earth as the Christian's hope (2 Pet. 3:13). Finally, the book of Revelation includes a glorious vision of the end of the present universe and the

---

[58] It is unwise to speak of the written Word of God as if it were of human origin, saying 'OT authors express the belief,' when what was written is the meaning and message of what God wanted to convey by means of the human author.

creation of a new universe, full of righteousness and the presence of God. The vision is confirmed by God in the awesome declaration: "I am making everything new!" (Rev. 21:1-8)

The new heavens and the new earth will be the renewed creation that will fulfill the purpose for which God created the universe. It will be characterized by the complete rule of God and by the full realization of the final goal of redemption: "Now the dwelling of God is with men" (Rev. 21:3).

The fact that the universe will be created anew[59] shows that God's goals for humans is not an ethereal and disembodied existence, but a bodily existence on a perfected earth. The scene of the beatific vision is the new earth. The spiritual does not exclude the created order and will be fully realized only within a perfected creation. (Elwell 2001, 828-29)

What have we learned so far in this publication? God created the earth to be inhabited, to be filled with perfect humans, who are over the animals, and under the sovereignty of God. (Gen 1:28; 2:8, 15; Ps 104:5; 115:16; Eccl 1:4) Sin did not

---

[59] Create anew does not mean a complete destruction followed by a re-creation, but instead a renewal of the present universe.

dissuade God from his plans (Isa. 45:18); hence, he has saved redeemable humankind by Jesus ransom sacrifice. It seems that the Bible offers two hopes to redeemed humans, **(1) a heavenly hope**, or **(2) an earthly hope.** It also seems that those with the heavenly hope are limited in number, and are going to heaven to rule with Christ as kings, priests, and judges either **on** the earth or **over** the earth from heaven. It seems that those with the earthly hope are going to receive everlasting life here on a paradise earth as originally intended.

GLOSSARY of Bible Terms

Dead. A composition, lyrical or musical, expressing deep sorrow, such as the grief expressed because of the death of a friend or a loved one; a lamentation.—2Sa 1:17; Ps 7:Sup.

Eternal. The Hebrew word *ôlām* 439x, according to its context, carries the thought of hidden time, long, everlasting, forever, eternity; from of old, ancient, lasting, for a duration, and times indefinite. The Greek word *aion´* 121 x, according to context, denotes a period of time that is indefinite, eternity, age, the present age, forever, forever and ever, and time indefinite.

Gehenna. Hebrew Ge' Hinnom, literally, valley of Hinnom appears 12 times in the Greek New Testament books, and many translators render it by the word "hell." Most translations have chosen poorly not to use a transliteration, Gehenna or Geenna, as opposed to the English hell, ASV, AT, RSV, ESV, LEB, HCSB, and NASB. There is little doubt that the New Testament writers and Jesus used "Gehenna" to speak of the place of final punishment. What was Gehenna?

According to the *Holman Illustrated Bible Dictionary* (p. 632), Gehenna or the Valley of Hinnom was "the valley south of Jerusalem now called the Wadi er-Rababi (Josh. 15:8; 18:16; 2 Chron. 33:6; Jer. 32:35) became the place of child sacrifice to foreign gods. The Jews later used the valley for the dumping of refuse, the dead bodies of animals, and executed criminals."[60] We would disagree with the other comments by the Holman Illustrated Dictionary, "The continuing fires in the valley (to consume the refuse and dead bodies) apparently led the people to transfer the name to the place where the wicked dead suffer." This just is not the case.

In the Old Testament, the Israelites did burn sons in the fires as part of a sacrifice to false gods, but not for the purpose of punishment, or torture. By the time of the New Testament period, hundreds of years later, the only thing thrown in Gehenna was trash and the dead bodies of executed criminals. For what purpose were these thrown into Gehenna? It was used as an incinerator, a furnace for destroying things by burning them. Notice that any bodies thrown in Gehenna during the New Testament period were already dead. Thus, if anything, these people saw Gehenna as a place where they destroyed their trash and the bodies of dead criminals. Thus, if Jesus used this to illustrate the place of the wicked, it would have represented destruction as the punishment.

Grave. When lowercased, referring to an individual grave; when capitalized, the common grave of mankind, equivalent to the Hebrew "Sheol" and the Greek "Hades." It is described in

---

60

http://biblia.com/books/hlmnillbbldict/Page.p_632

the Bible as a symbolic place or condition wherein all activity and consciousness cease.—Ge 47:30; Ec 9:10; Ac 2:31.

Hades. Everyone knows that Hades was "the underground abode of the dead in Greek mythology."[61] However, as far as early Christianity, the Greek translation of the Old Testament, the Septuagint, uses the word Hades 73 times, employing it 60 times to translate the Hebrew word Sheol. Luke at Acts 2:27 write, "For you will not abandon my soul to Hades, or let your Holy One see corruption." Luke was quoting Psalm 16:10, which reads, "For you will not abandon my soul to Sheol, or let your holy one see corruption." Notice that Luke used Hades in place of Sheol. Therefore, Hades is the Greek equivalent of Sheol, as far as Christians and the Greek New Testament is concerned. In other words, Hades is also the abode of the dead in early Christian thought. Some translations choose to use a transliteration, Hades, as opposed to the English hell, ASV, AT, RSV, ESV, LEB, HCSB, and NASB.

Hell. Without being bogged down in doctrinal issues, let us just deal with the facts. "Hell" is the English translation for the Hebrew word Sheol and the Greek word Hades. Therefore, we need not ask, what Hell is. However, what did the word mean when it was first placed in English translations? Webster's Eleventh New International Dictionary,

---

[61] http://biblia.com/books/mwdict11/word/hades

under "Hell" says: [Middle English, from Old English; akin to Old English helan to conceal, Old High German helan, Latin celare, Greek kalyptein] before 12th century"[62] The word "hell" meant to 'cover' over or 'conceal,' so it would have meant a place 'covered' or 'concealed,' such as a grave.

Lake of fire. A symbolic place that "burns with fire and sulfur," also described as "the second death." Unrepentant sinners, the Devil, and even death and the Grave (or, Hades) are thrown into it. The inclusion of a spirit creature and also of death and Hades, all of which cannot be affected by fire, indicates that this lake is a symbol, not of everlasting torment, but of everlasting destruction.—Re 19:20; 20:14, 15; 21:8.

Resurrection. The Greek word *anastasis* 42x, depending on the context means raising up; standing up, resurrection. – Ac 24:15; Php 3:11; Re 20:5-6; John 5:28-29; 11:25.

Sheol. Webster's Dictionary, "[Hebrew *Shĕ'ōl*] 1597: the abode of the dead in early Hebrew thought"[63] Collier's Encyclopedia (1986, Vol. 12, p. 28) says: "Since Sheol in Old Testament times referred simply to the abode of the dead and suggested no moral distinctions, the word 'hell,' as understood today, is not a happy translation." Some translations choose to use a transliteration,

---

[62] http://biblia.com/books/mwdict11/word/hell

[63] http://biblia.com/books/mwdict11/word/sheol

Sheol, as opposed to the English hell, AT, RSV, ESV, LEB, HCSB, and NASB. – Gen. 37:35; Ps 16:10; Ac 2:31.

OTHER BOOKS IN THIS SERIES

WHO IS THE ANTICHRIST

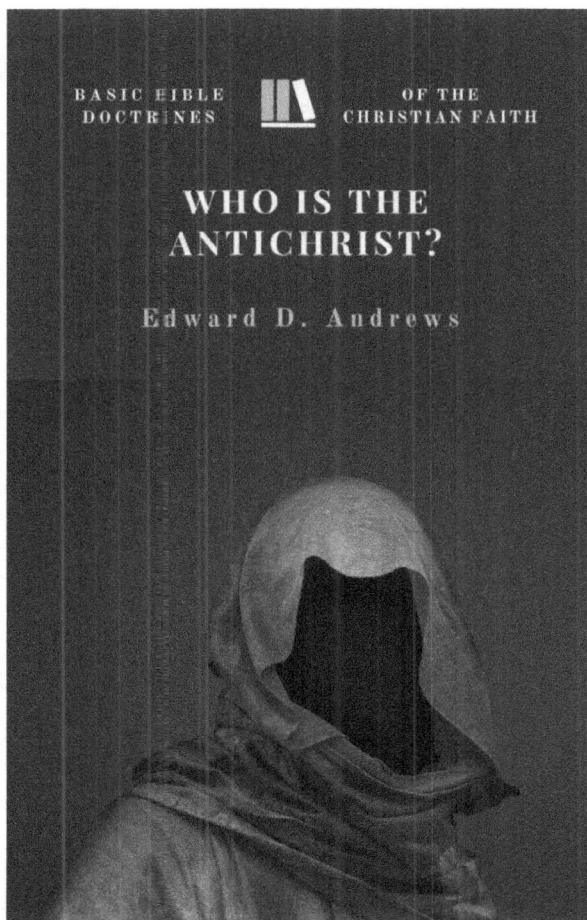

WHERE ARE THE DEAD?

BASIC BIBLE DOCTRINES   OF THE CHRISTIAN FAITH

WHERE ARE THE DEAD?

Edward D. Andrews

The SECOND COMING of CHRIST

BASIC BIBLE DOCTRINES

OF THE CHRISTIAN FAITH

The SECOND COMING of CHRIST

Edward D. Andrews

BASIC BIBLE DOCTRINES · OF THE CHRISTIAN FAITH

EXPLAINING THE DOCTRINE OF MAN

Edward D. Andrews

BASIC BIBLE
DOCTRINES

OF THE
CHRISTIAN FAITH

EXPLAINING THE HOLY SPIRIT

Edward D. Andrews

Bibliography

Anders, Max, and Doug McIntosh. *Holman Old Testament Commentary - Deuteronomy (pp. 359-360).* . Nashville: B&H Publishing, 2009.

Brand, Chad, Charles Draper, and England Archie. *Holman Illustrated Bible Dictionary: Revised, Updated and Expanded.* Nashville, TN: Holman, 2003.

Bratcher, Robert G., and Howard Hatton. *A Handbook on the Revelation to John.* New York: United Bible Societies, 1993.

Bromiley, Geoffrey W., and Gerhard Friedrich. *Theological Dictionary of the New Testament, ed. Gerhard Kittel, vol. 4.* Grand Rapids, MI: Eerdmans, 1964-.

Bullinger, Ethelbert William. *Figures of Speech Used in the Bible.* London; New York: E. & J. B. Young & Co., 1898.

Elwell, Walter A. *Evangelical Dictionary of Theology (Second Edition).* Grand Rapids: Baker Academic, 2001.

Erickson, Milliard J. *Christian Theology.* Grand Rapids, MI: Baker Academic, 1998.

Gangel, Kenneth O. *Holman New Testament Commentary, vol. 4, John .* Nashville, TN: Broadman & Holman Publishers, 2000.

Geisler, Norman L., and Thomas Howe. *The Big Book of Bible Difficulties*. Grand Rapids: Baker Books, 1992.

Kittel, Gerhard, Gerhard Friedrich, and Geoffrey William Bromiley. *Theological Dictionary of the New Testament*. Grand Rapids: Eerdmans, 1995, c1985.

Knight, George W. *The Pastoral Epistles: A Commentary on the Greek Text, New International Greek Testament Commentary*. Grand Rapids, MI; Carlisle, England: W.B. Eerdmans; Paternoster Press, 1992.

Lea, Thomas D. *Holman New Testament Commentary: Vol. 10, Hebrews, James*. Nashville, TN: Broadman & Holman Publishers, 1999.

McReynolds, Paul R. *Word Study: Greek-English*. Carol Stream: Tyndale House Publishers, 1999.

Mounce, William D. *Mounce's Complete Expository Dictionary of Old & New Testament Words*. Grand Rapids, MI: Zondervan, 2006.

Stein, Robert H. *A Basic Guide to Interpreting the Bible: Playing by the Rules*. Grand Rapids: Baker Books, 1994.

Thomas, Robert L. *Revelation 1-7: An Exegetical Commentary* . Chicago, IL: Moody Publishers, 1992.

—. *Revelation 8-22: An Exegetical Commentary* . Chicago, IL: Moody Publishers, 1995.

Towns, Elmer L. *Concise Bible Dictrines: Clear, Simple, and Easy-to-Understand Explanations of Bible Doctrines.* Chattanooga: AMG Publishers, 2006.

Vine, W E. *Vine's Expository Dictionary of Old and New Testament Words.* Nashville: Thomas Nelson, 1996.

Zodhiates, Spiros. *The Complete Word Study Dictionary: New Testament.* Chattanooga: AMG Publishers, 2000, c1992, c1993.

Zuck, Roy B. *Basic Bible Interpretation: A Prafctical Guide to Discovering Biblical Truth.* Colorado Springs: David C. Cook, 1991.